Earth's Vulnerabilities

Photography

Preface

"Vulnerability is the birthplace of innovation, creativity and change. Courage starts with showing up and letting ourselves be seen." "Vulnerability sounds like truth and feels like courage. Truth and courage aren't always comfortable, but they're never weakness"-Goodreads

The expression of vulnerabilities of emotions can give a sign with the mind of weakness but in this weakness, one can be open to the world of love and uniqueness inside of authentic self within a divine character. It's a character that can open things of weakness and bring strength to the world around them. I believe if everyone is suppressed in the notions of comfort and non-functional states of mind then, one must find the courage to be vulnerable to the world and show the expression of love from the unique viewpoint of its own character.

This unique character expresses the solid foundation of nature and the wisdom will show, as the growth inspires the one's on who can not see the past the darkest night, but one can seize an opportunity of blessing by being vulnerable.

Earth's vulnerabilities can showcase the simplest things to the most extreme cases of the outcomes of a human mind. The simplest thing can be a baby being born into this world and/or a seed growing into a flower. These simple pleasures can take the mind in many altered directions from something positive, but the hardest things come about, then the soul is sometimes driven to walk away from them on one level, until a clever and vulnerable person rises and challenges the viewpoints of those at the hardest level.

We can see these things coming through all directions in our lives, but the uniqueness within this book gives the viewer an option to be vulnerable and showcase courage with an optical point of view. This point of view is a personal journey within one's own self and make the clarity within. It gives a colorful spin to those having a hard day and a vulnerability of courage from an image point of view.

Life can make or break us at any time within our own lives but having the courage to stand up and be recognized through the eyes of mother earth. It's the honesty within her own beauty and the story telling she conveys to the humans on the vulnerabilities she is sharing within her DNA of life. She is showcasing the outcomes of weakness through the vulnerabilities but is also trying to convey humans need more courage to rise to each occasion of any outcome. She is simple but complex as we know it to be on earth.

This book expresses the journey of earth's vulnerabilities within a single lens point of view point but also sharing the hidden meanings and suggestions of the mentality of humans. It gives you all the room to grow and expand your own world but the expressions of my own character of vulnerabilities and showcase the true women that I am within.

Thank you for taking the time in rediscovering the earth's vulnerabilities through my own artwork of expressionism photography.

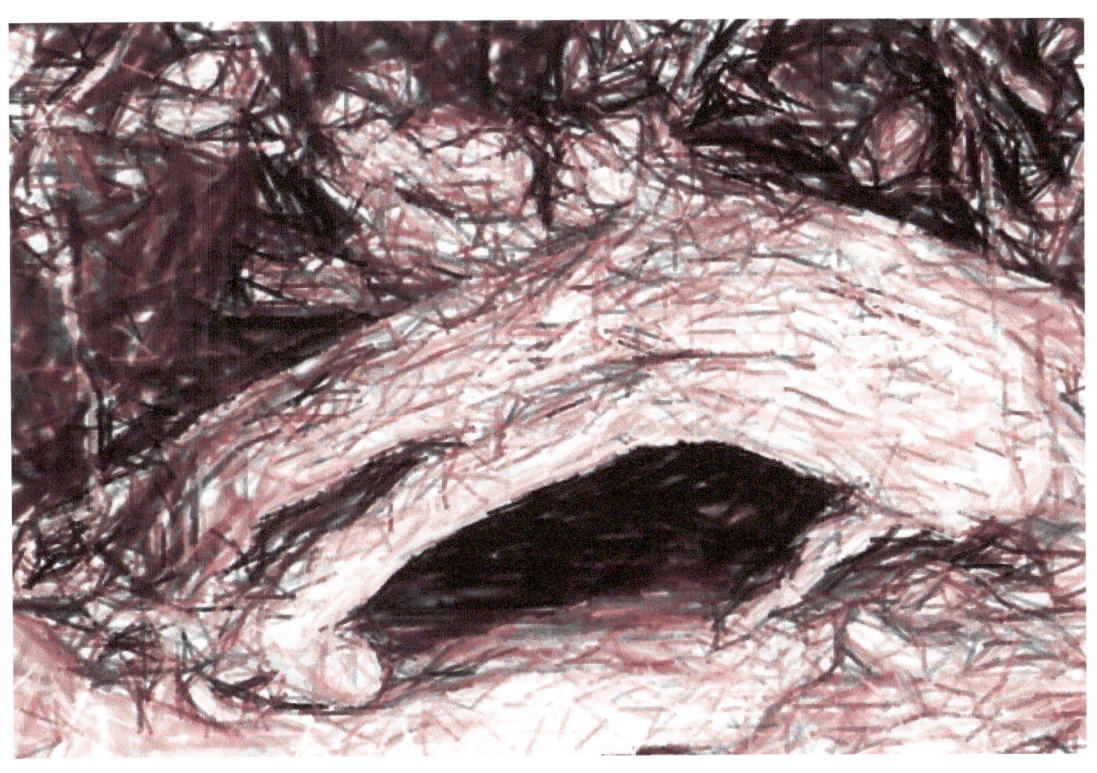

Earth Painted Hand in Nature

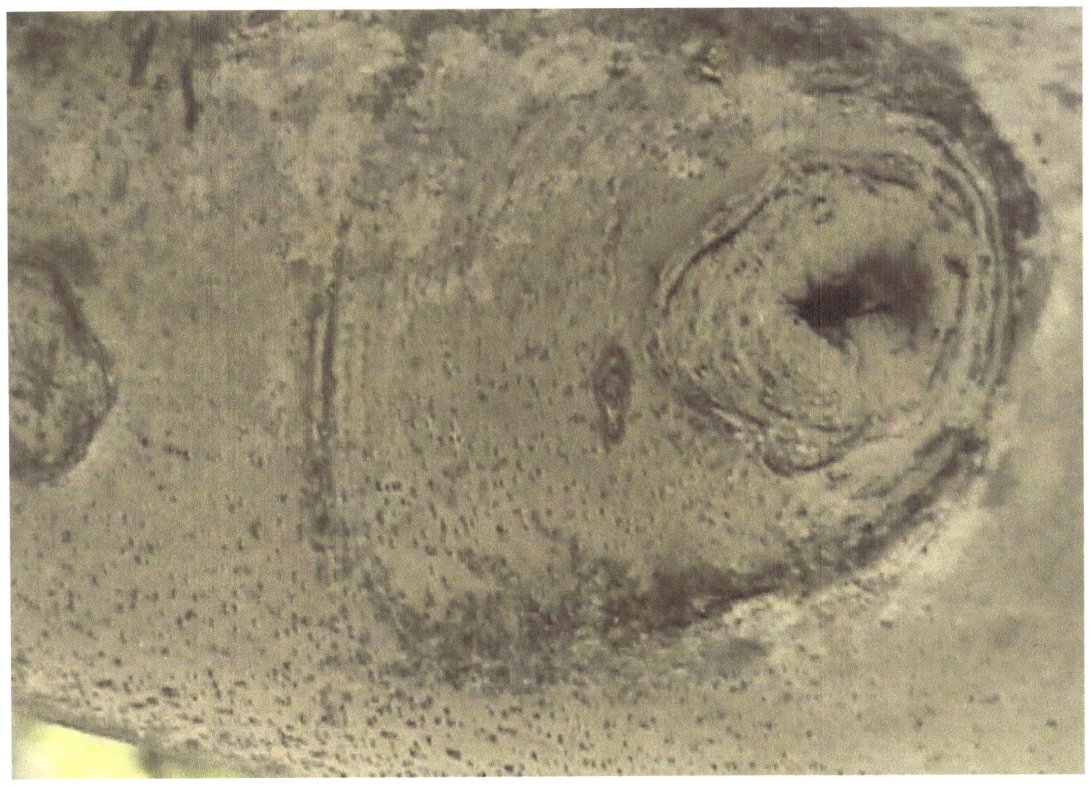

Tiny Opening

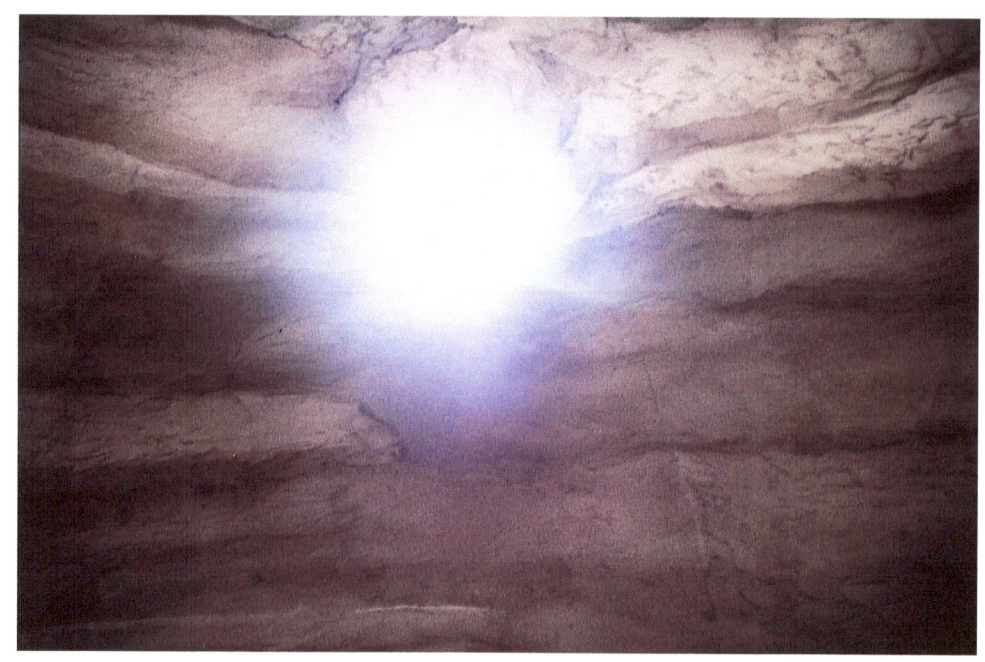

Layered Rocks Opened by the Sun

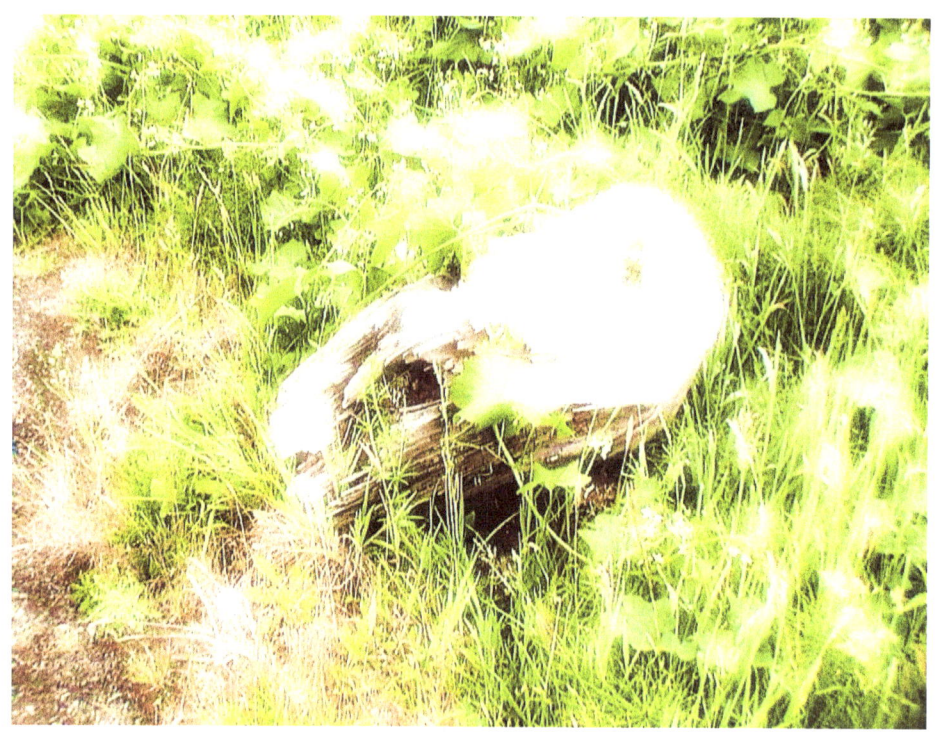

Etched Layers of Electricity

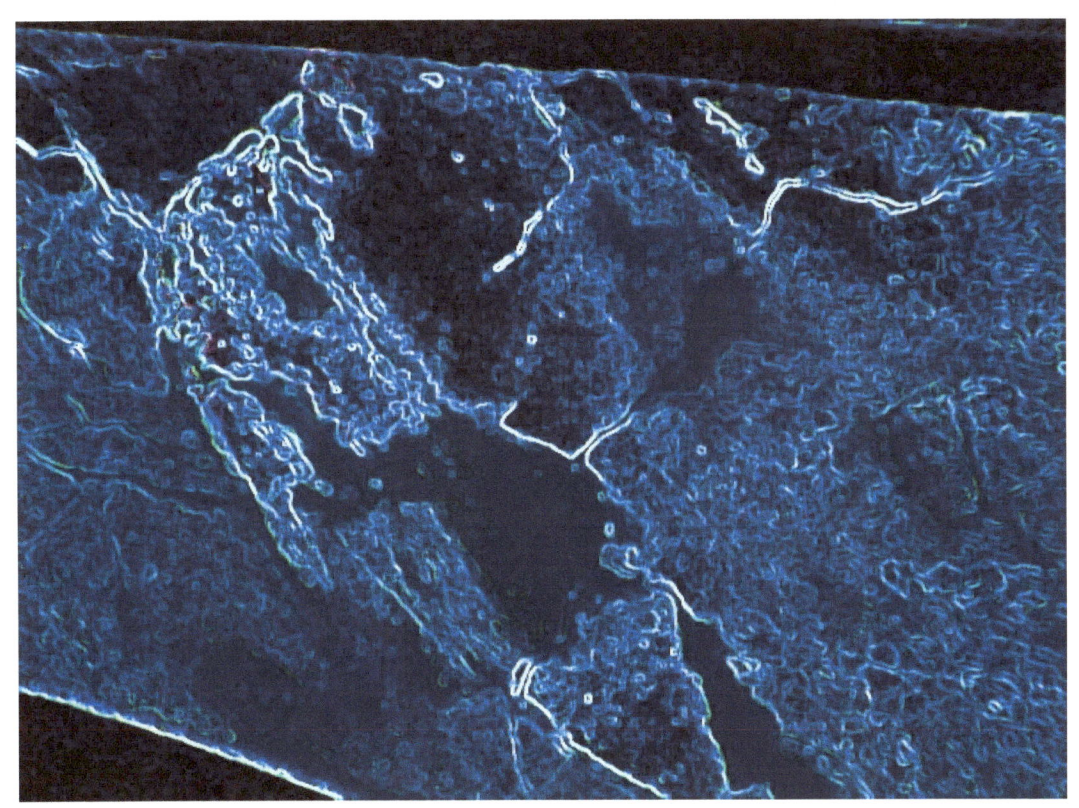

A Wall of Icey Blue

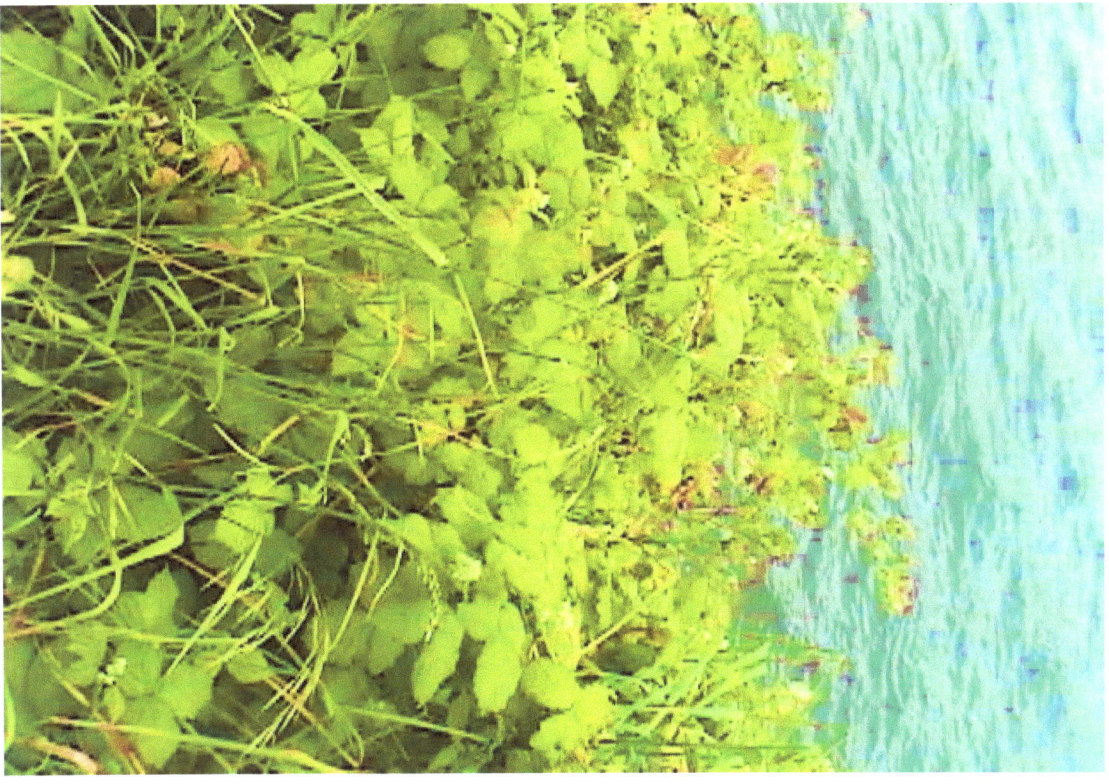

Earthly Water Blend

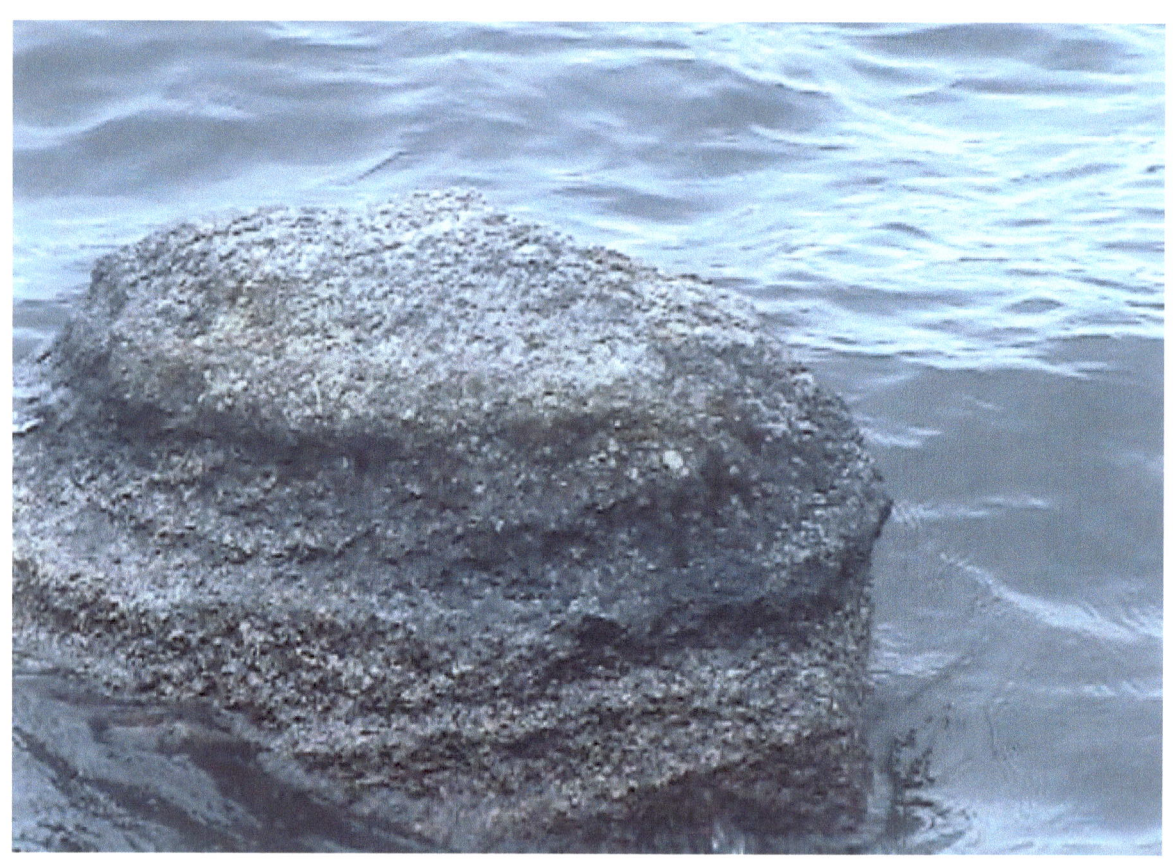

Solidarity

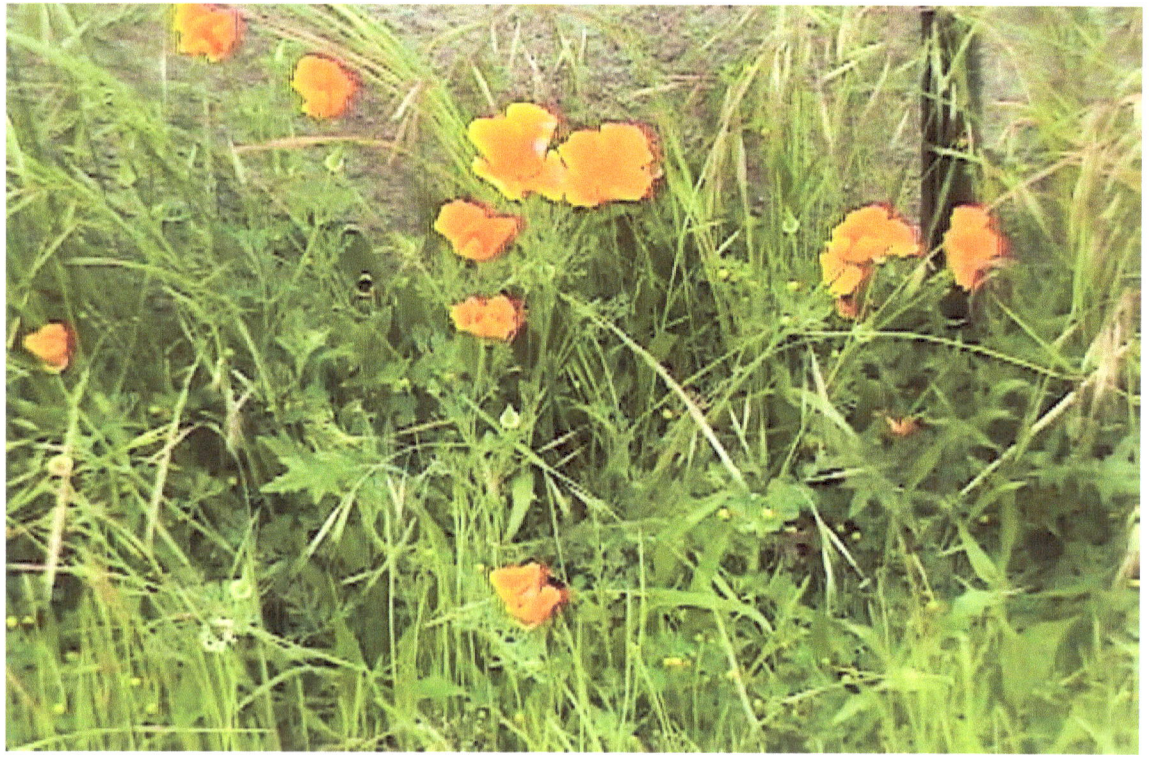

Optical Eye Confused

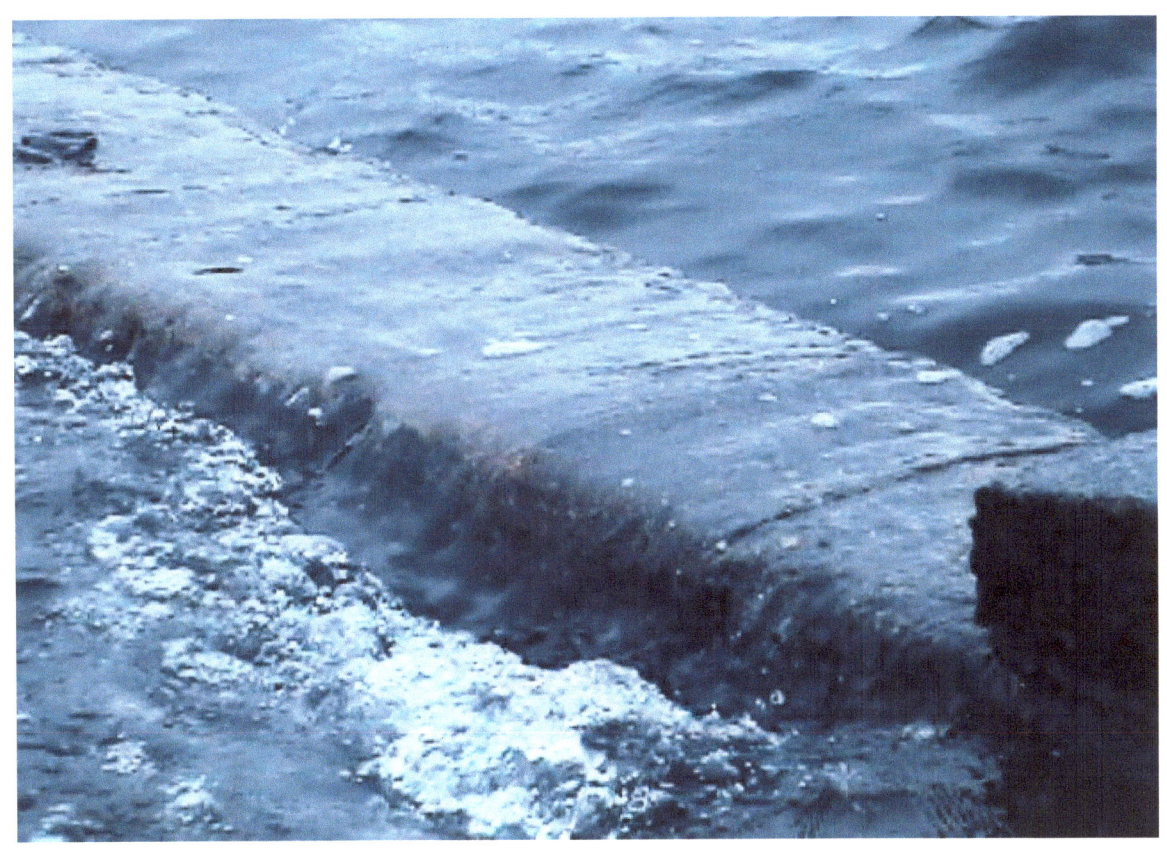

Exhilaration Flow

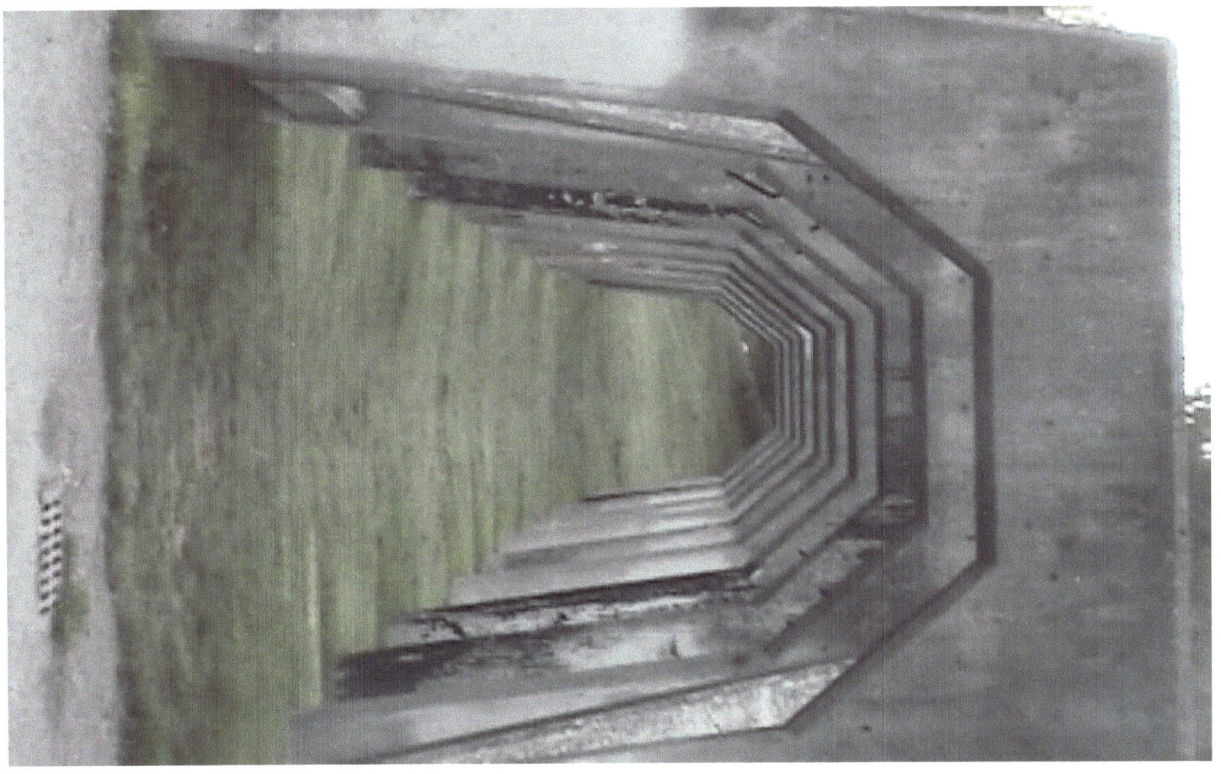

Obstacle Vision

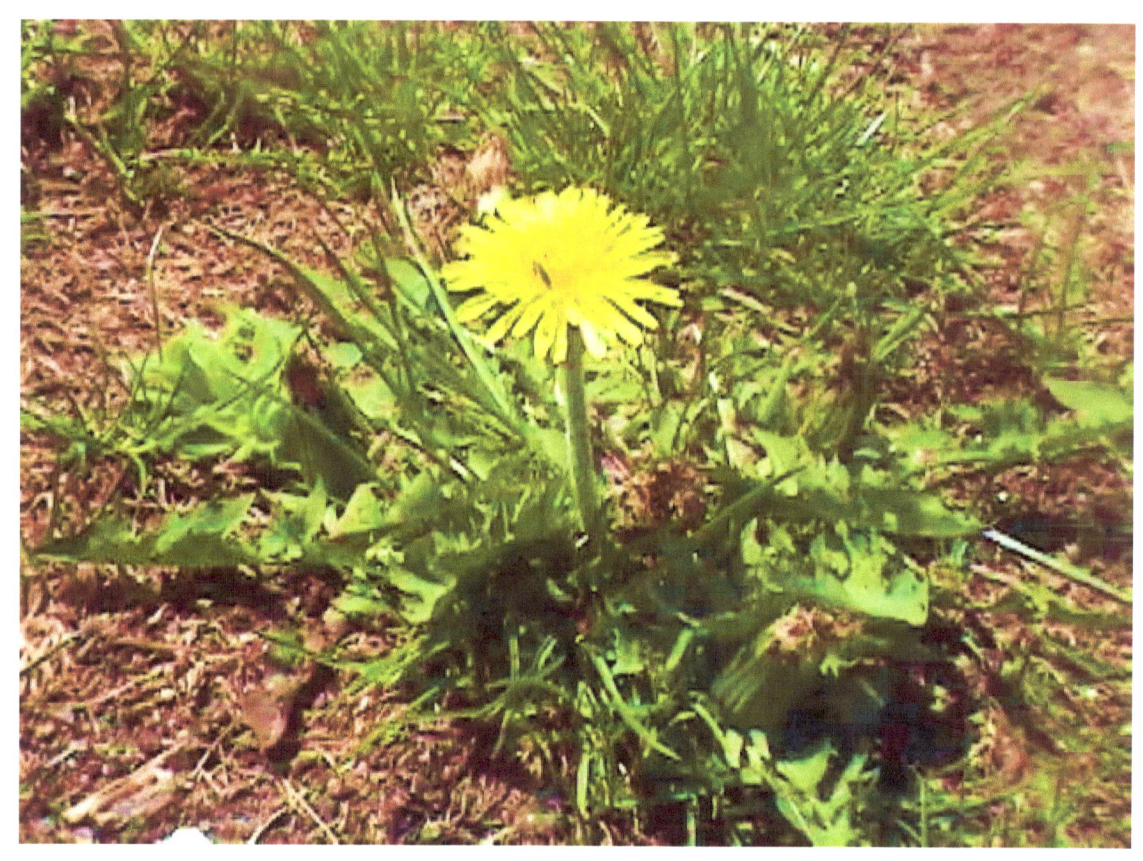

Oneness

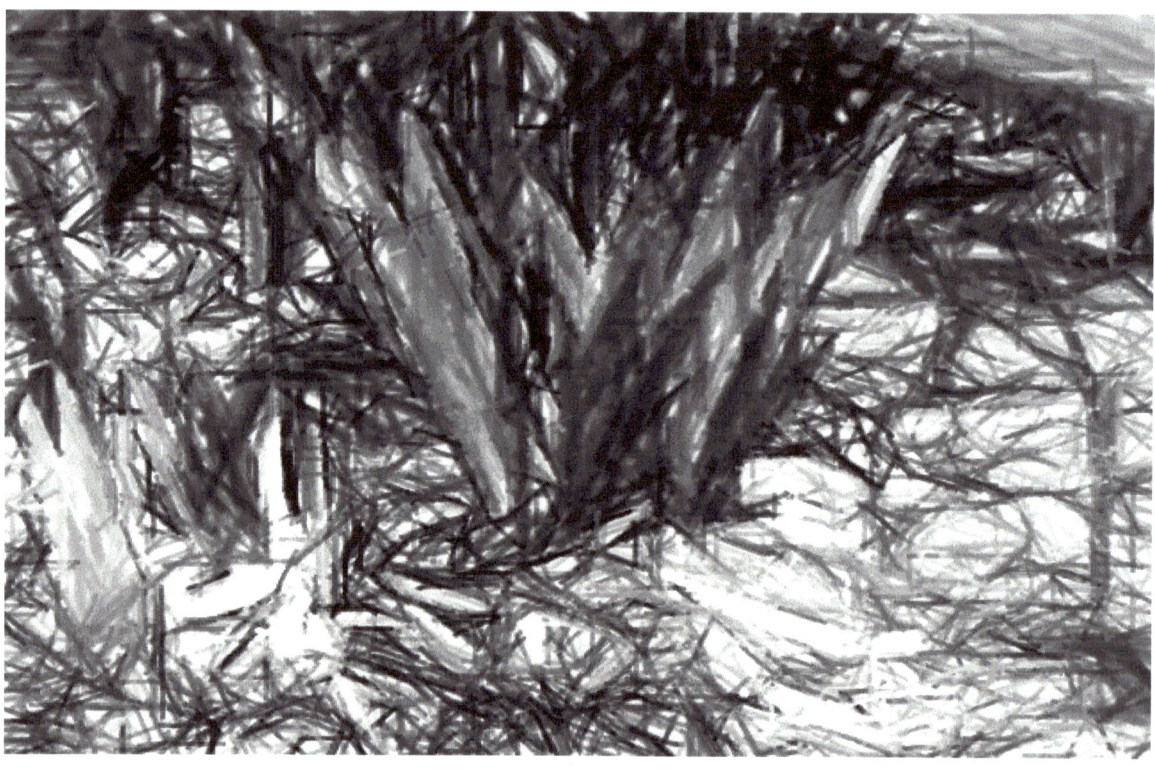

Curving through lines

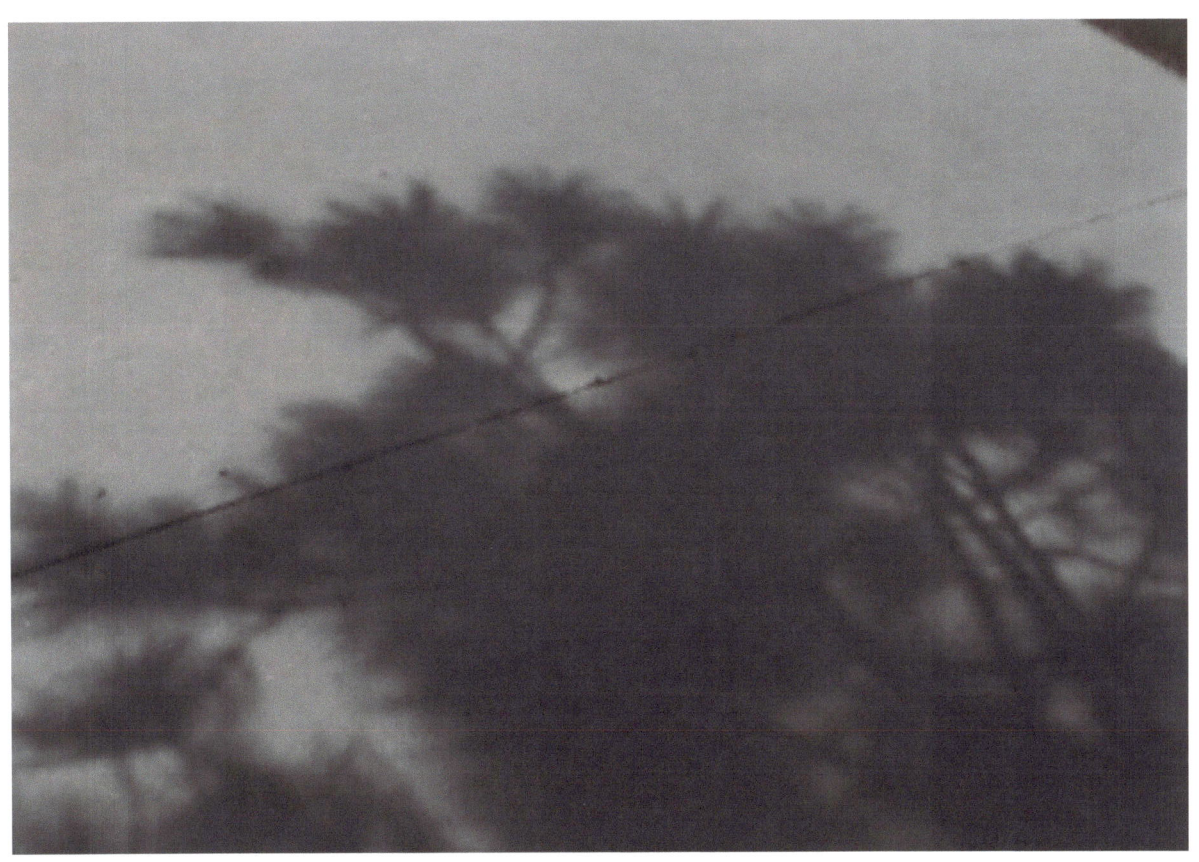

Two Hearts Connected

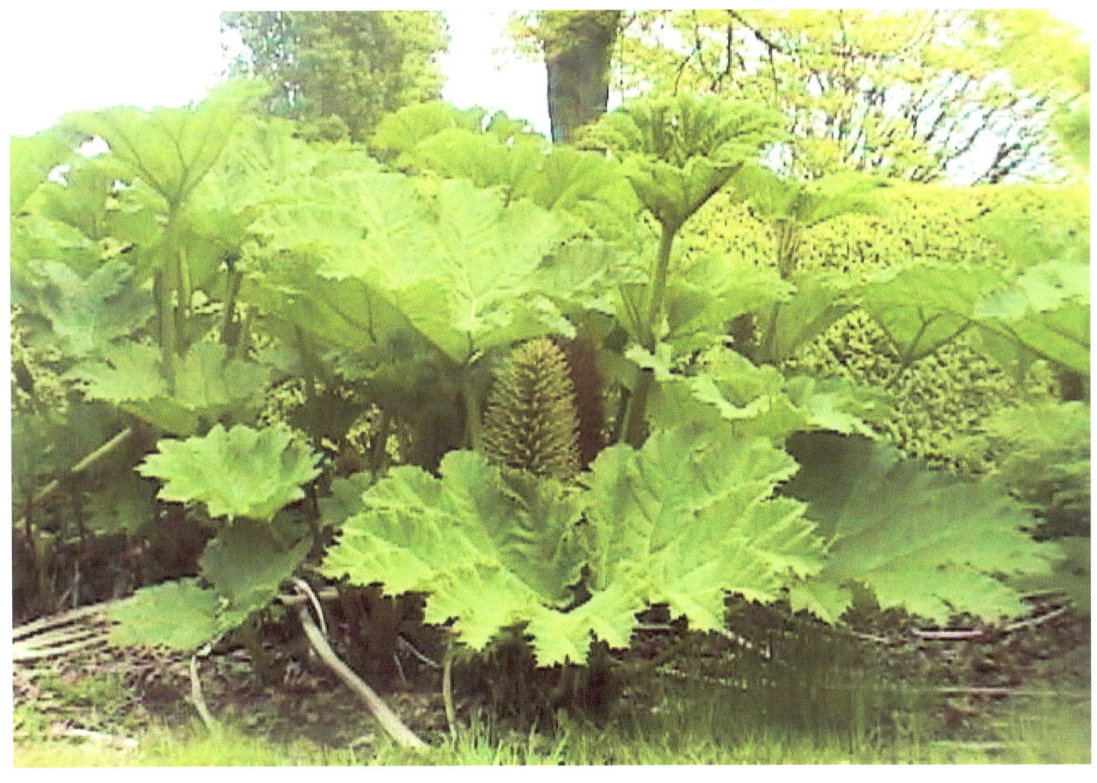

Root Grounding

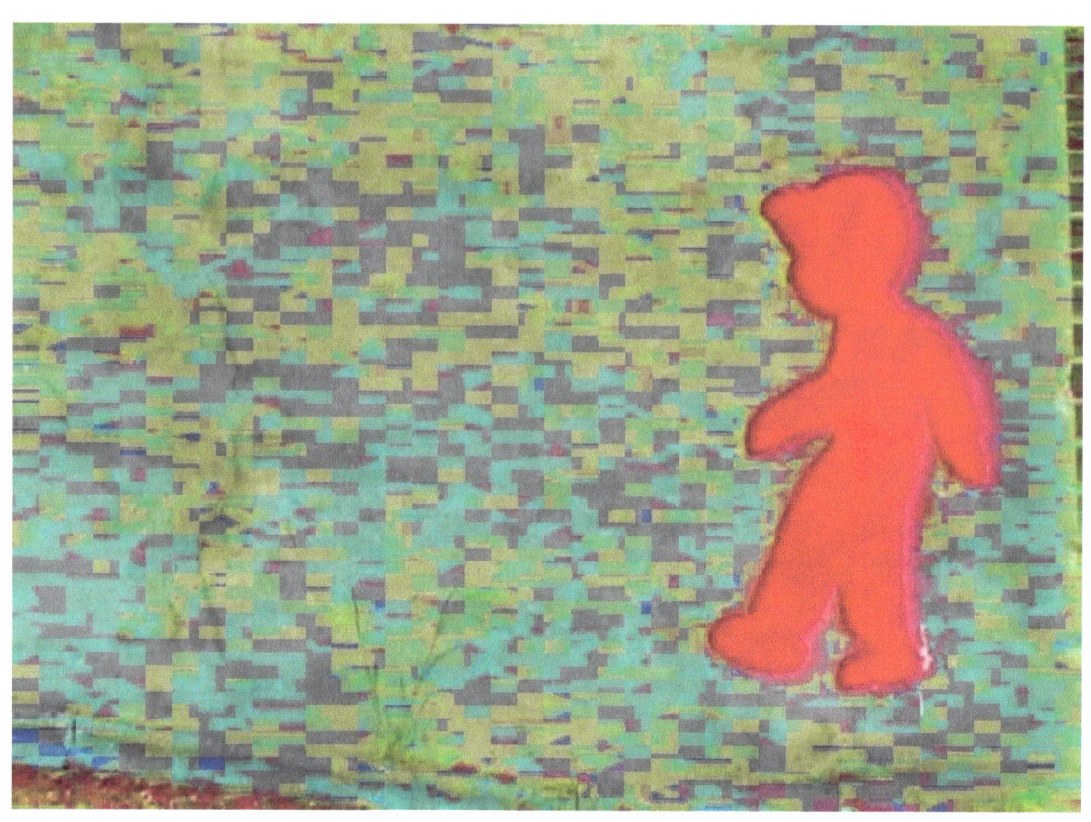

Inner Child Puzzle

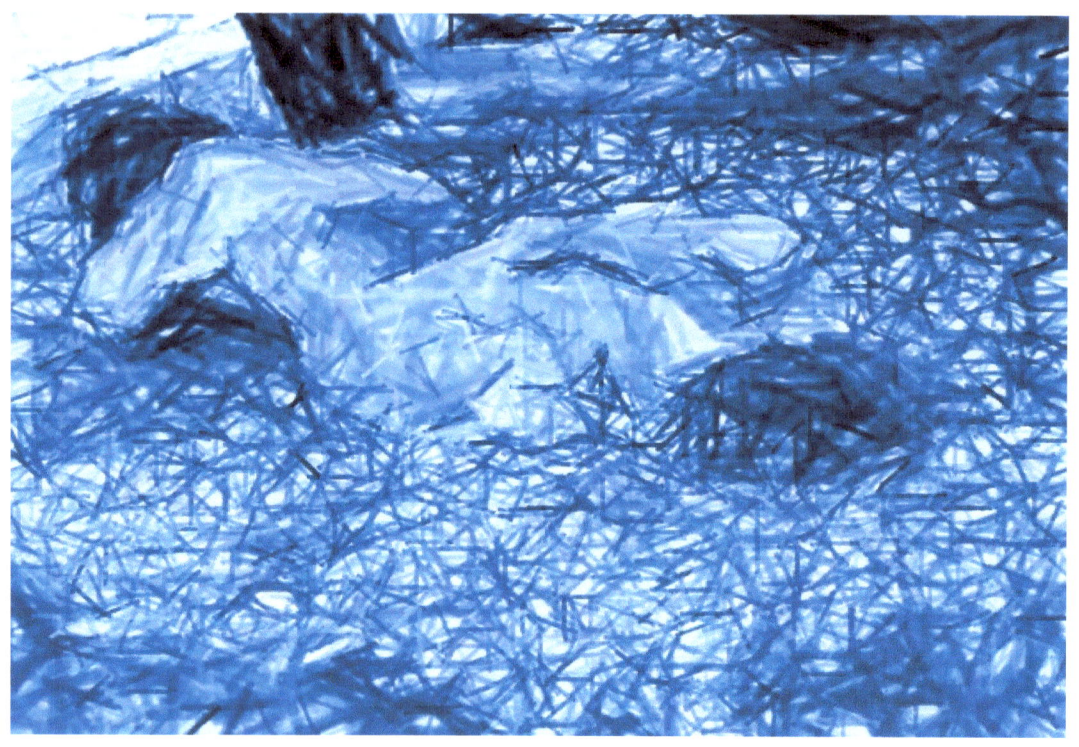

Hazy Blue Arrow

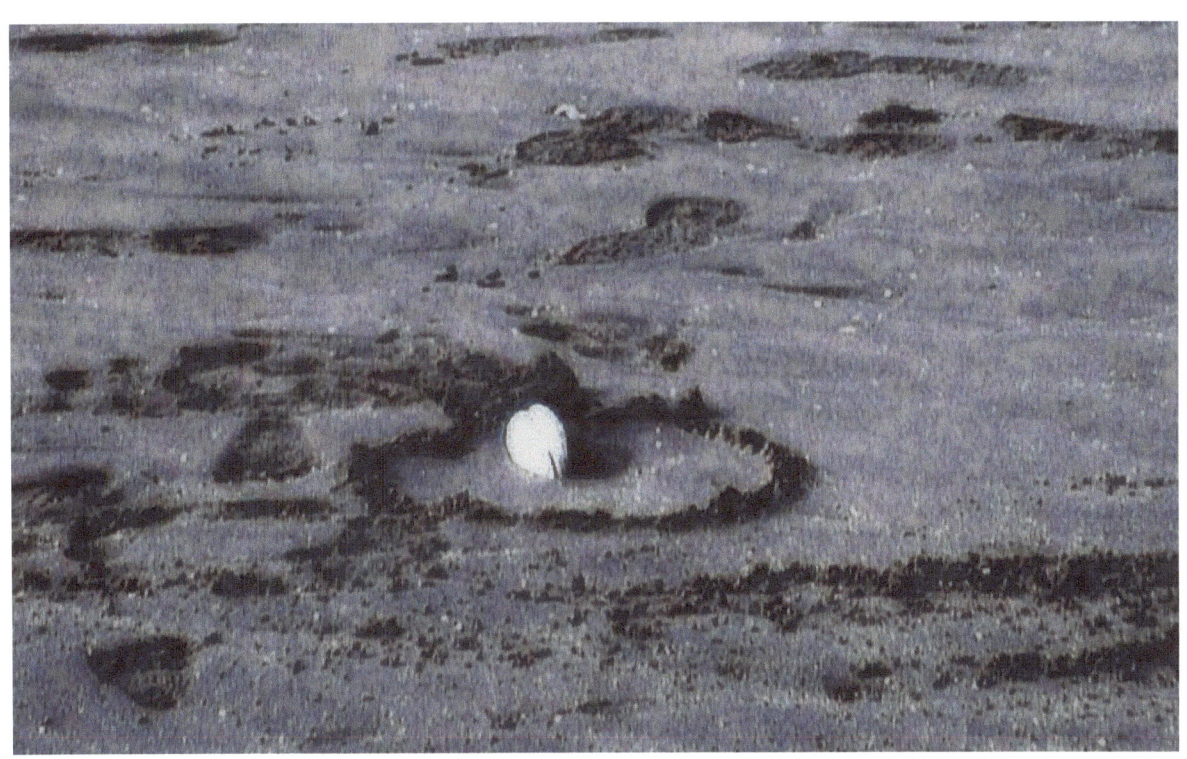

Silent Footsteps to the Center

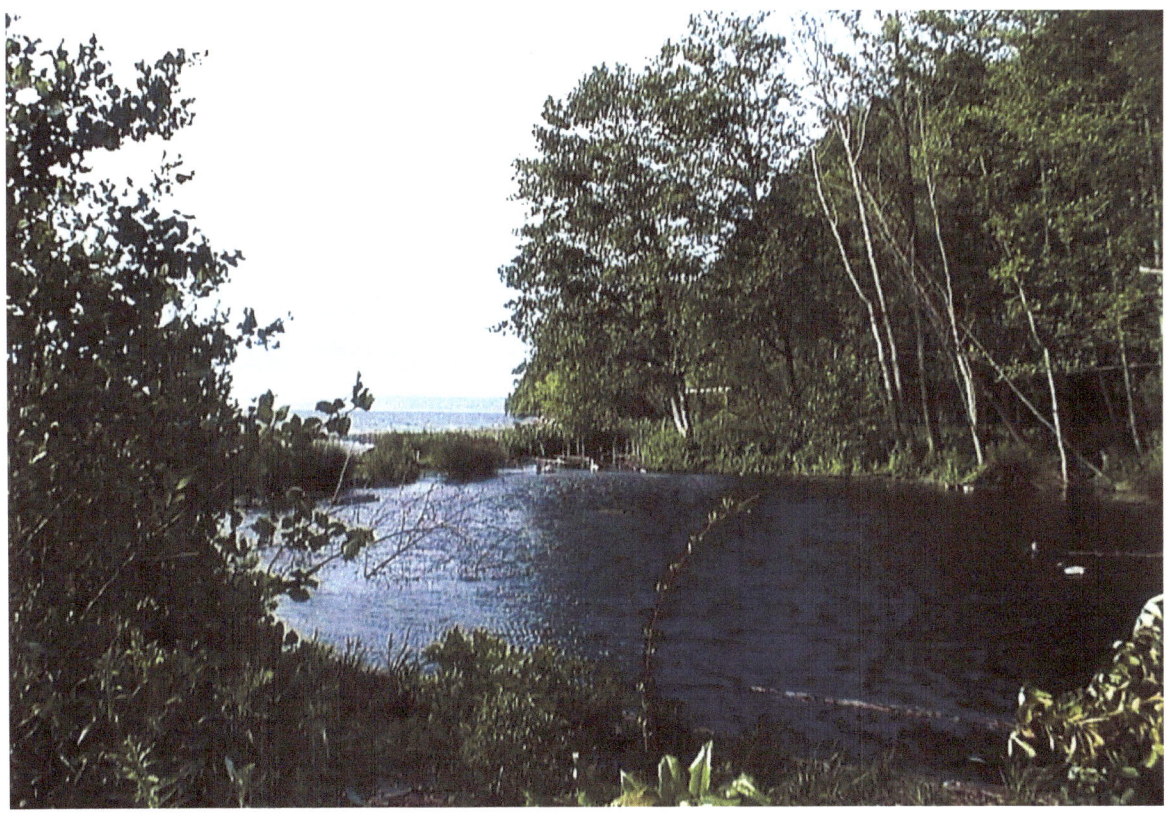

Off in the Distance

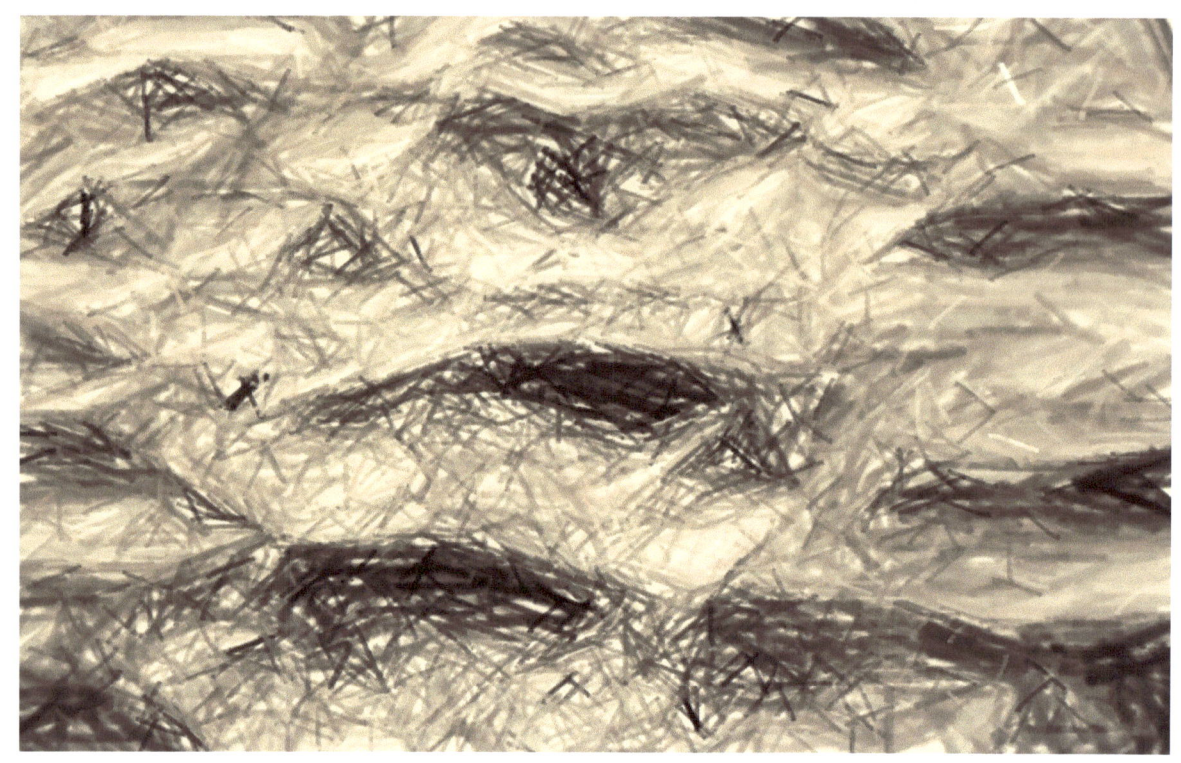

Layers of Gentleness

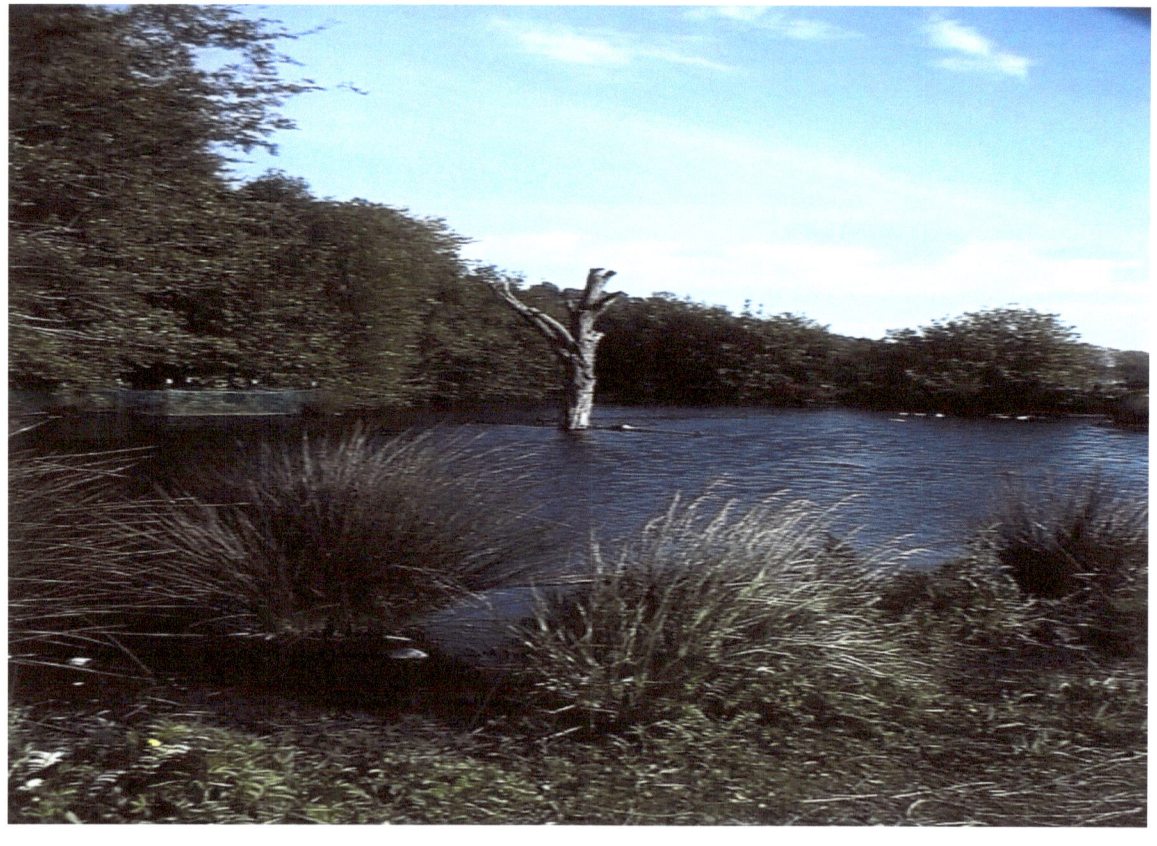

Breezy Emotions

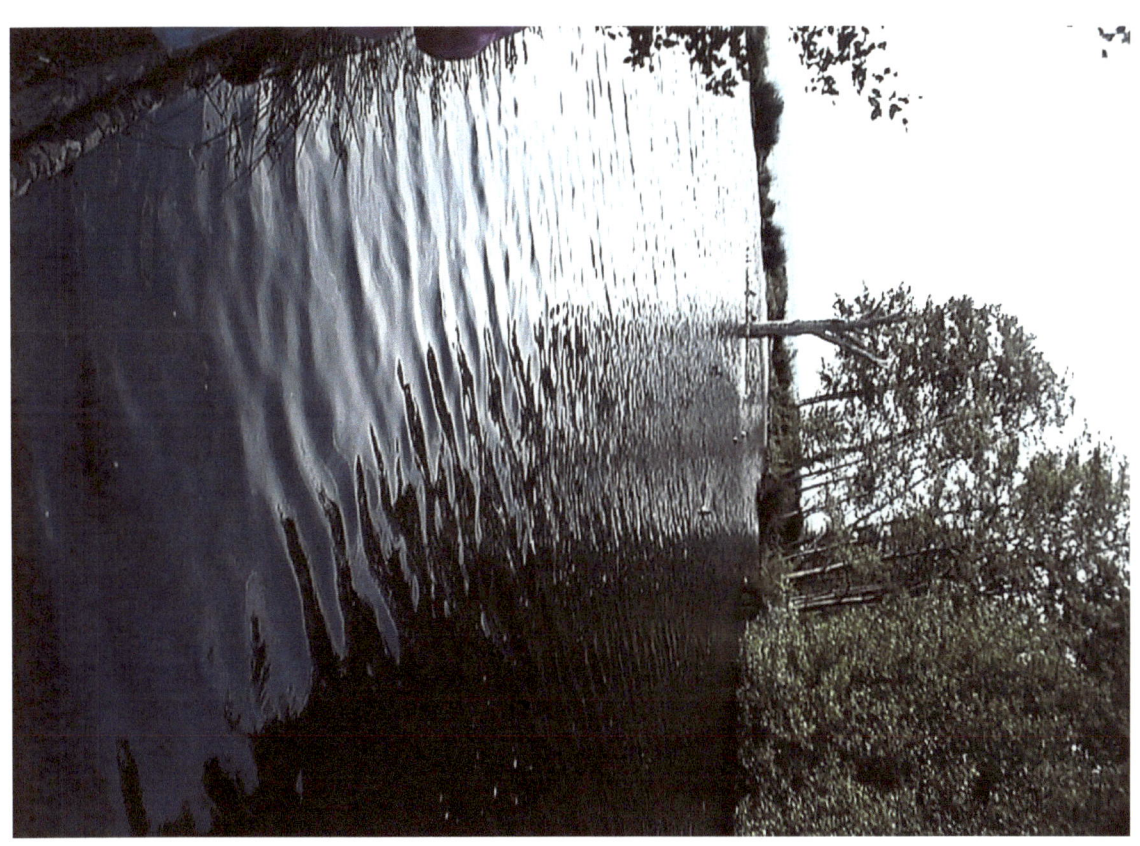

Cleaning Your Soul

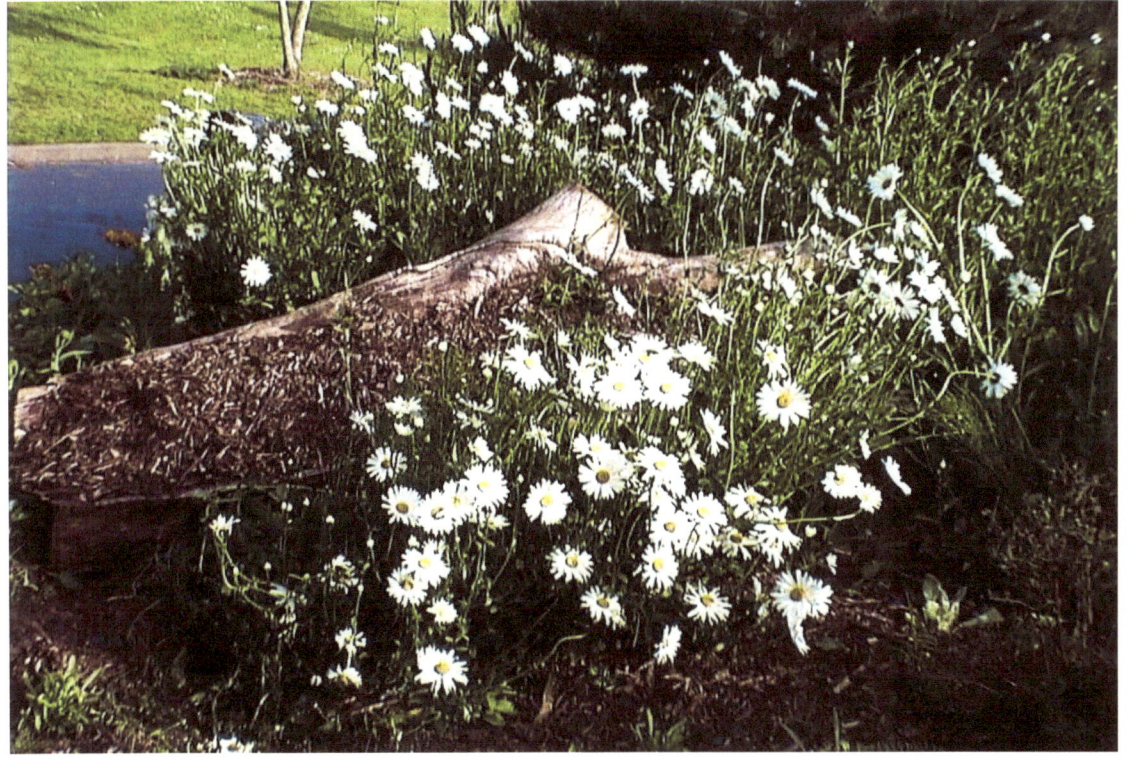

Shadow Strength

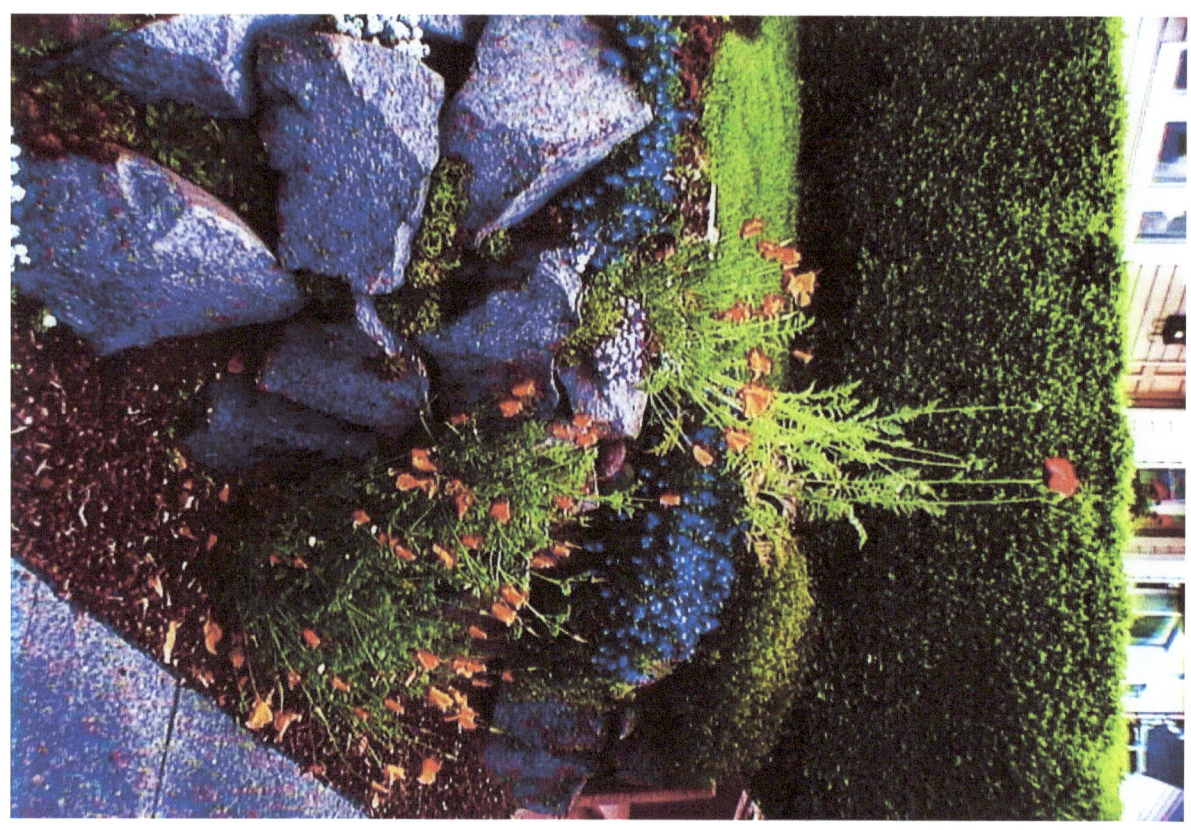

Strength Stretched Downward

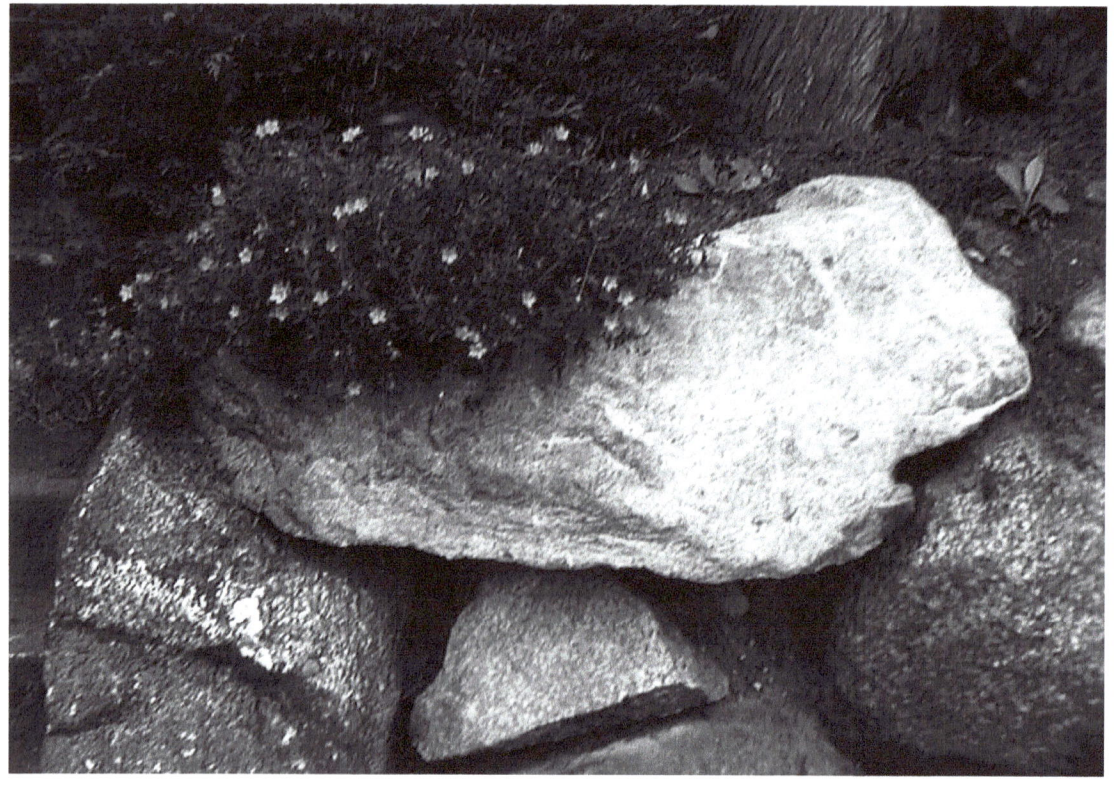

Eight Edges

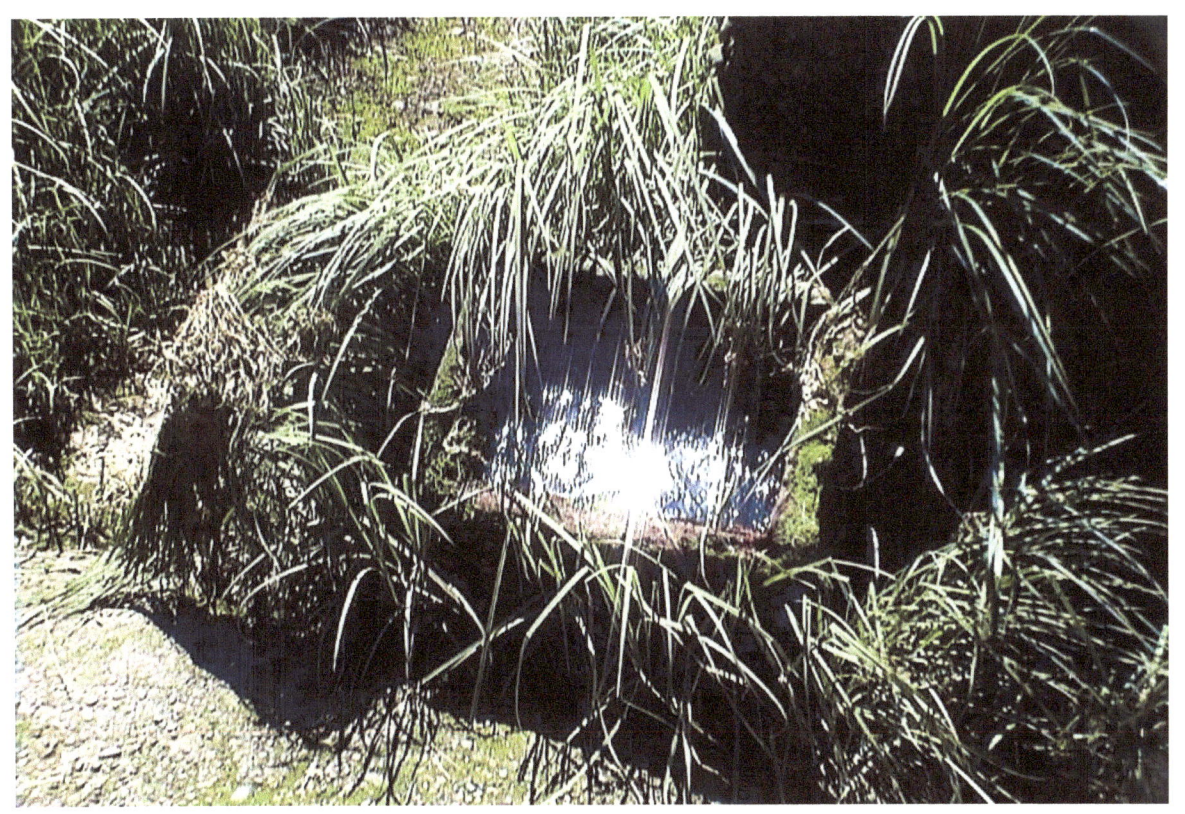

Crystal Light

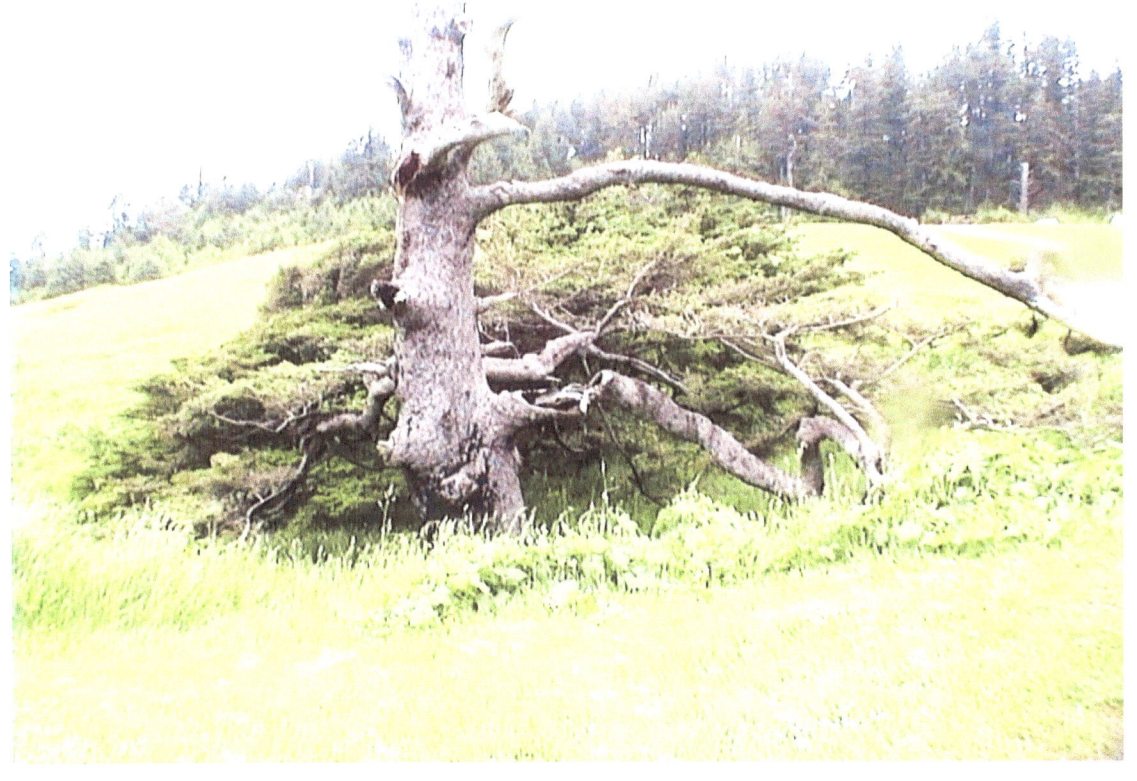

Open Female Arms

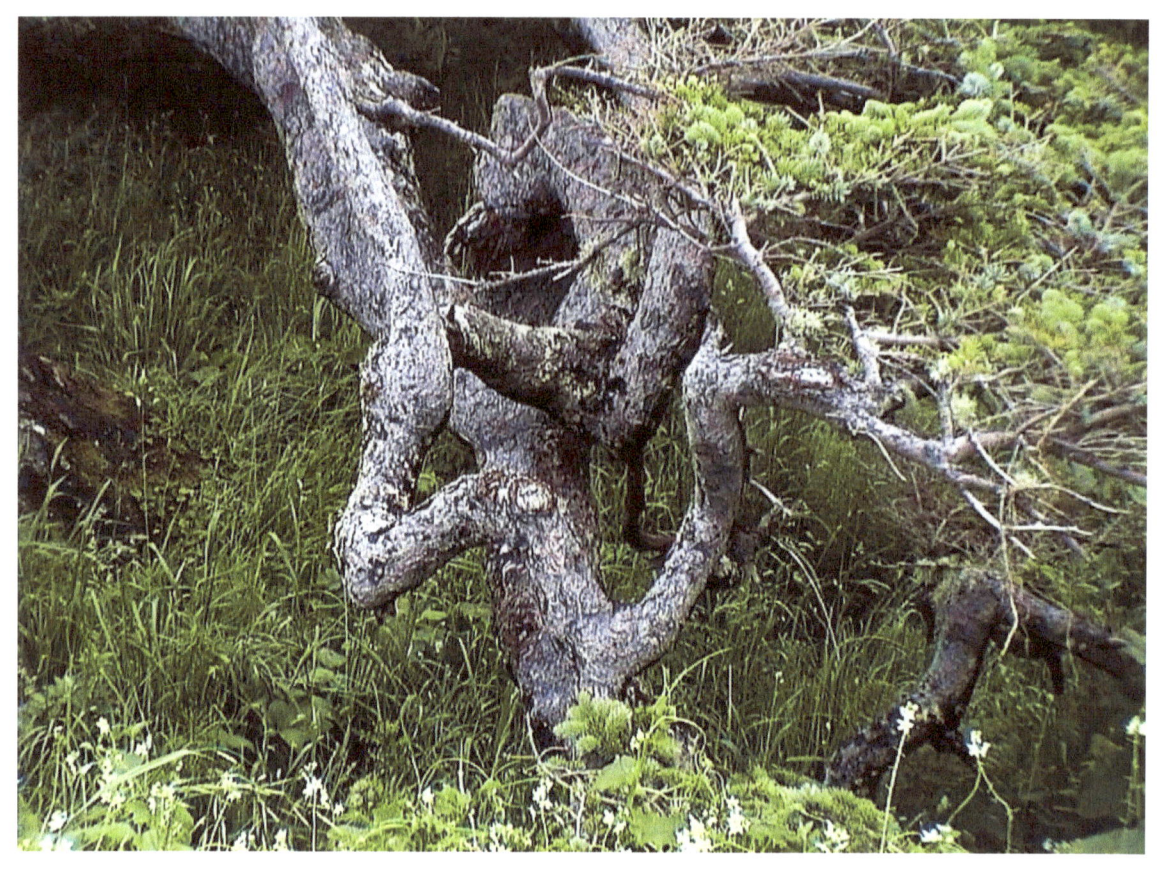
Tree Horse

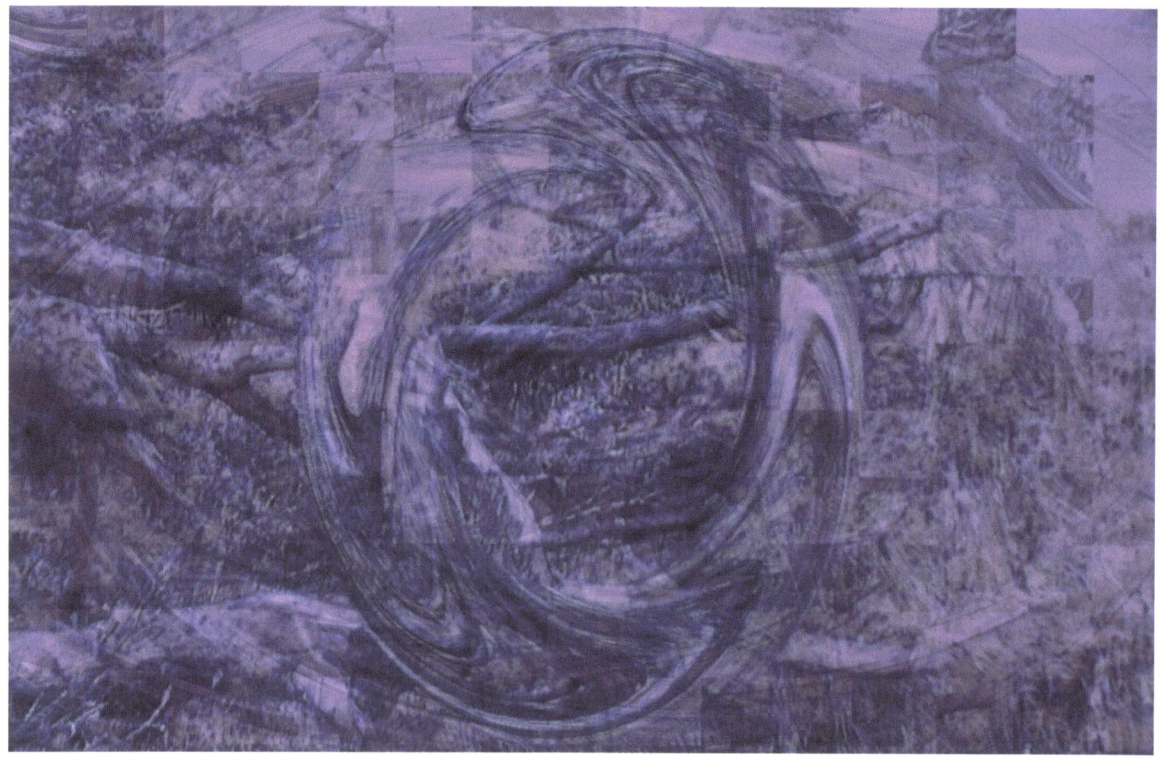
Logical Spin

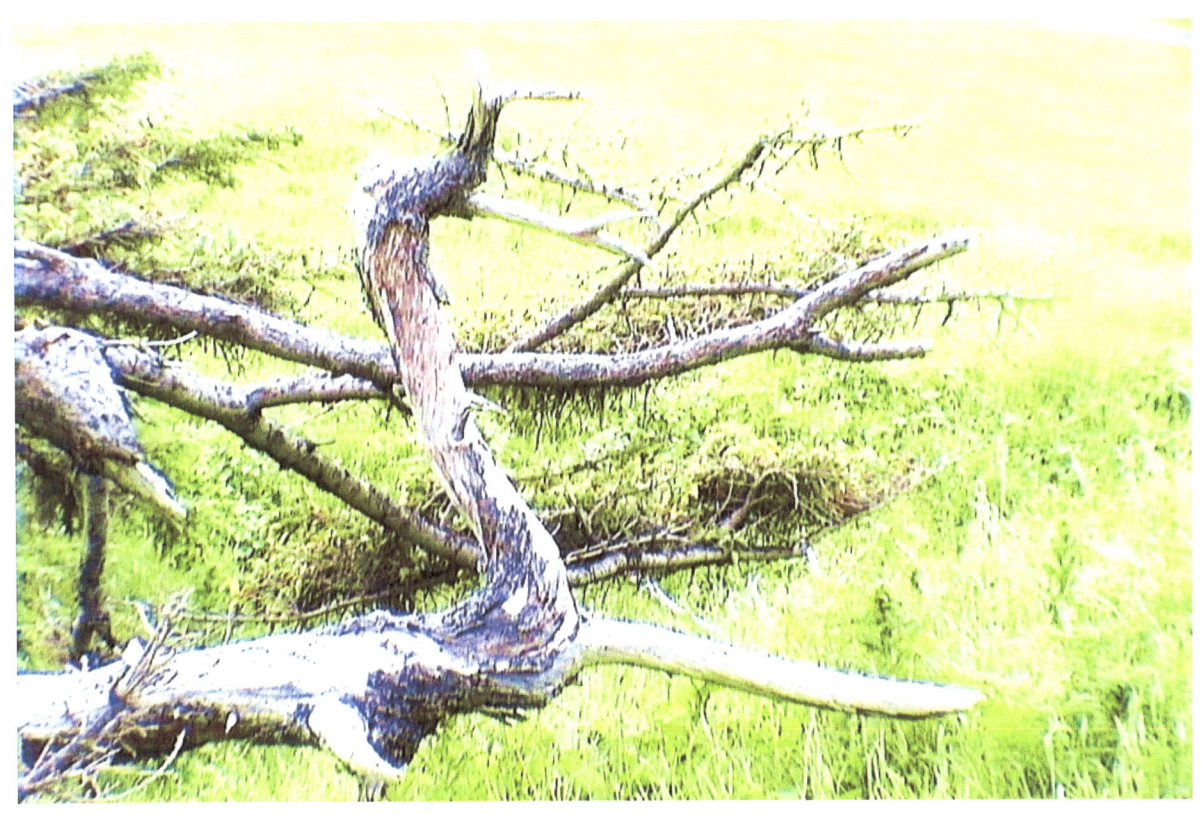

Branches of Color

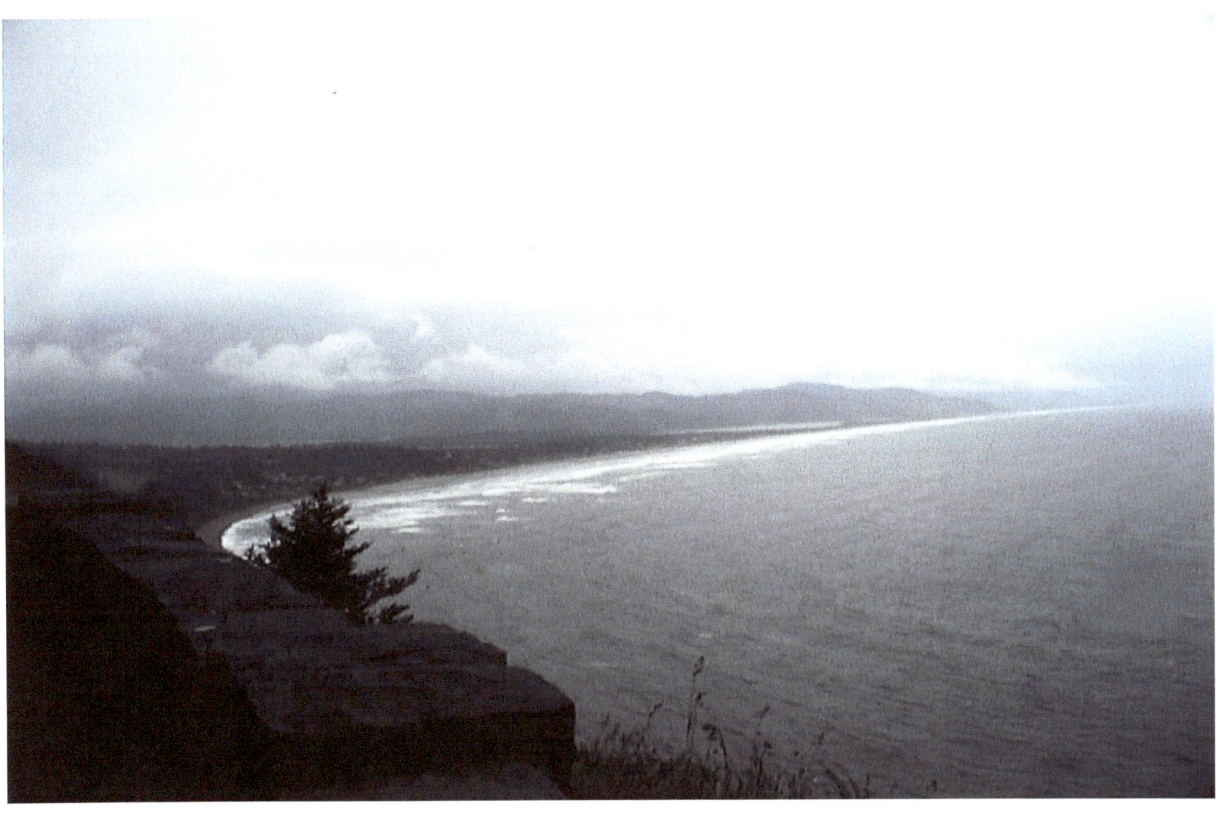

Curved Movement

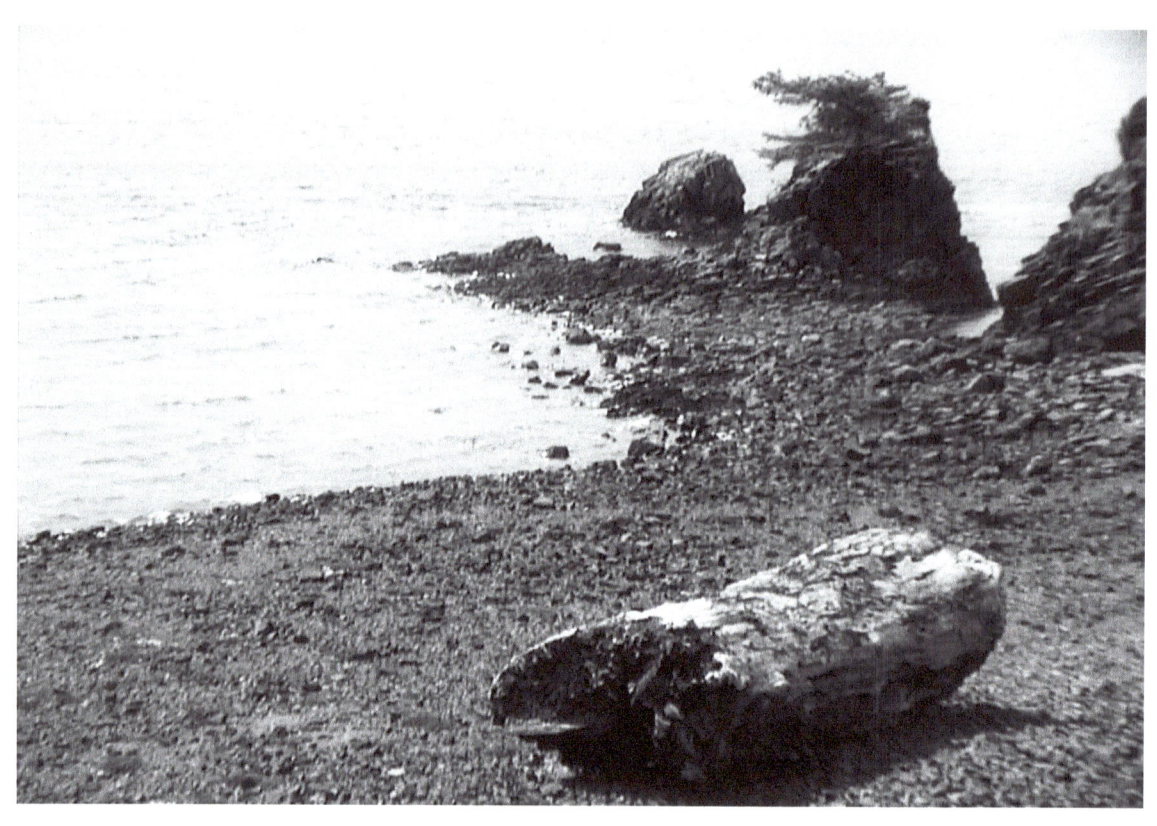

Story to Express

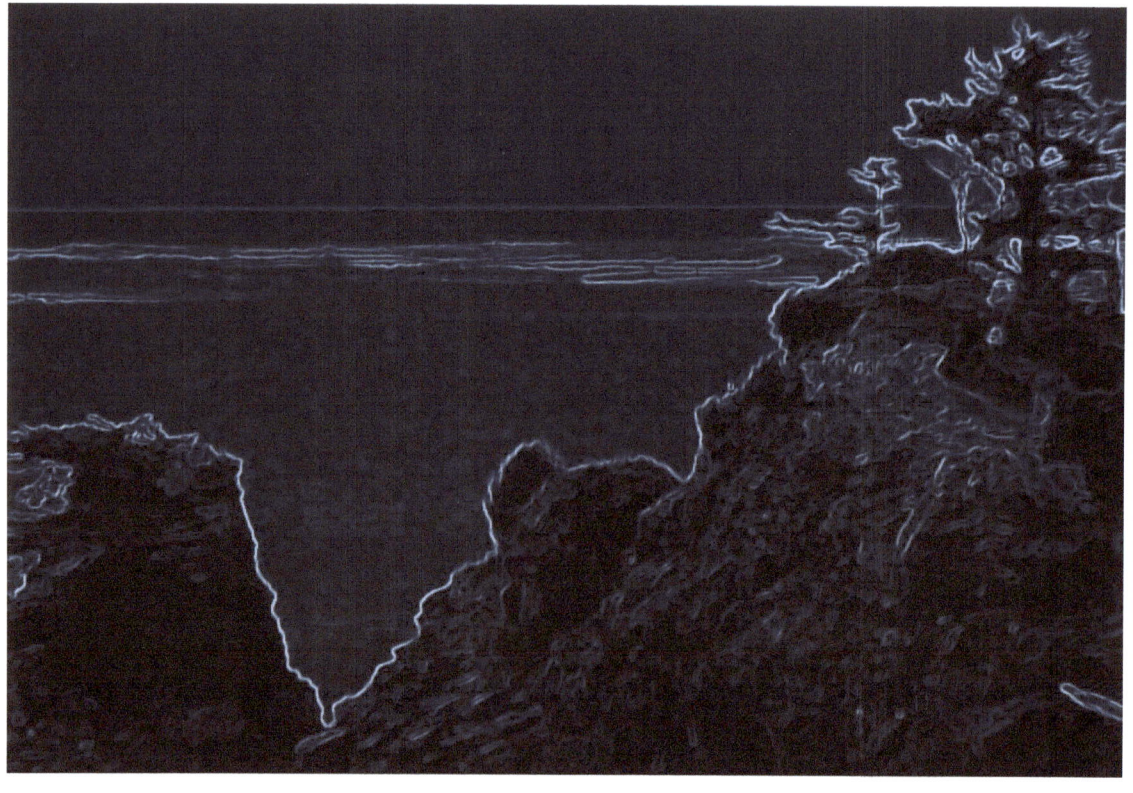

Sensational Lines

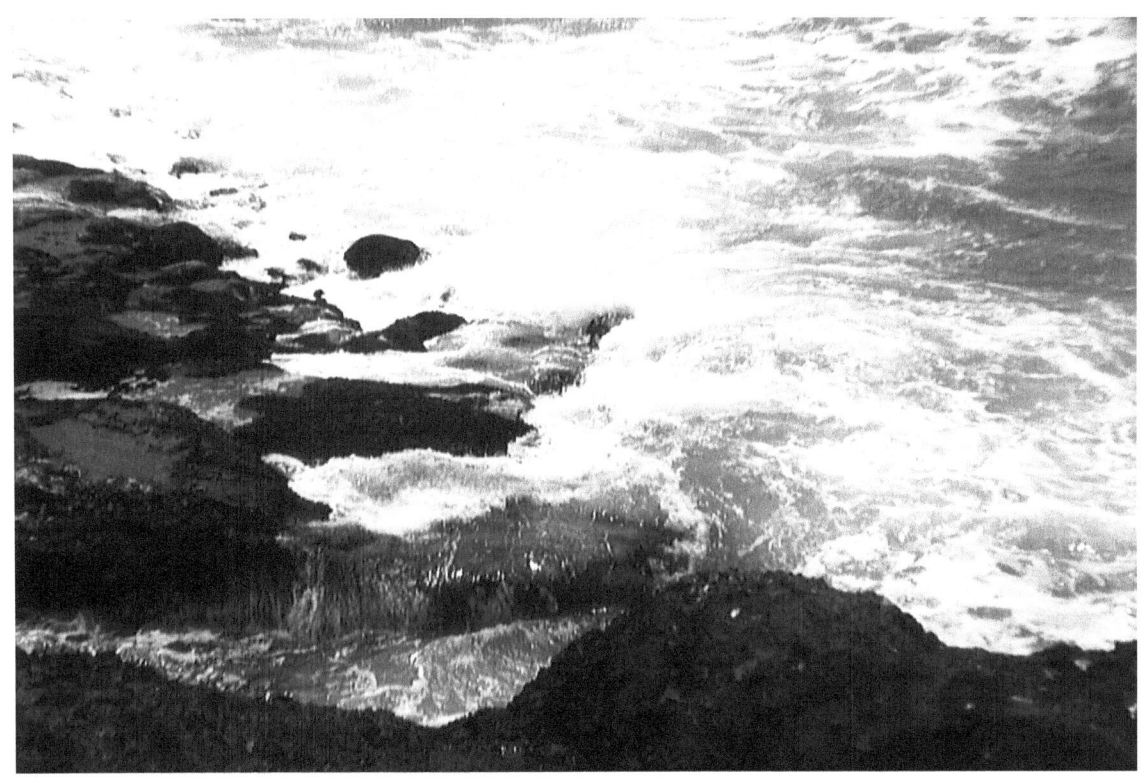

Ecstasy of Flow

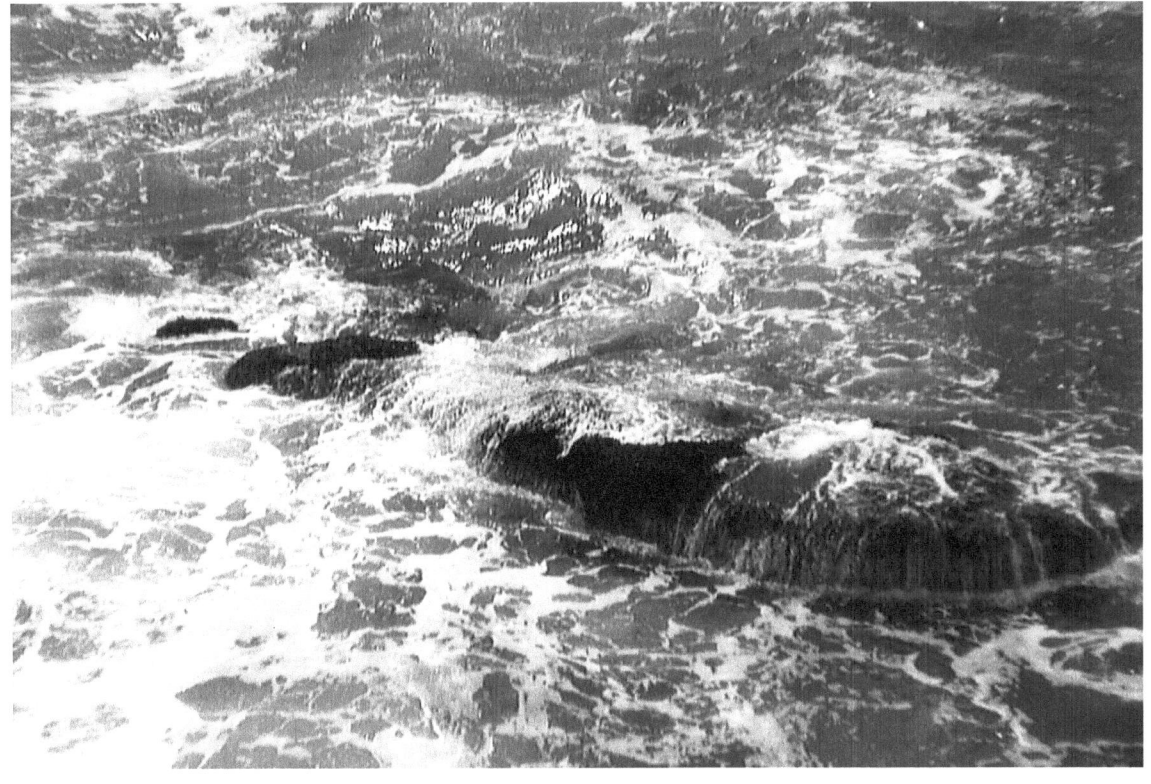

Pouring Over

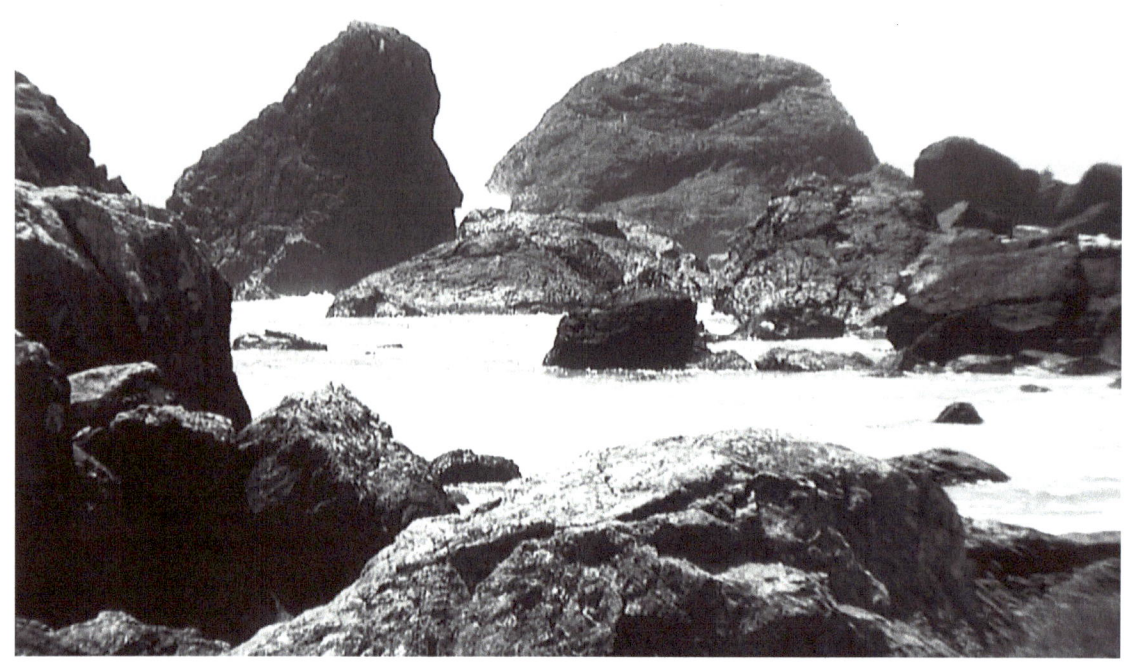

Firm Support

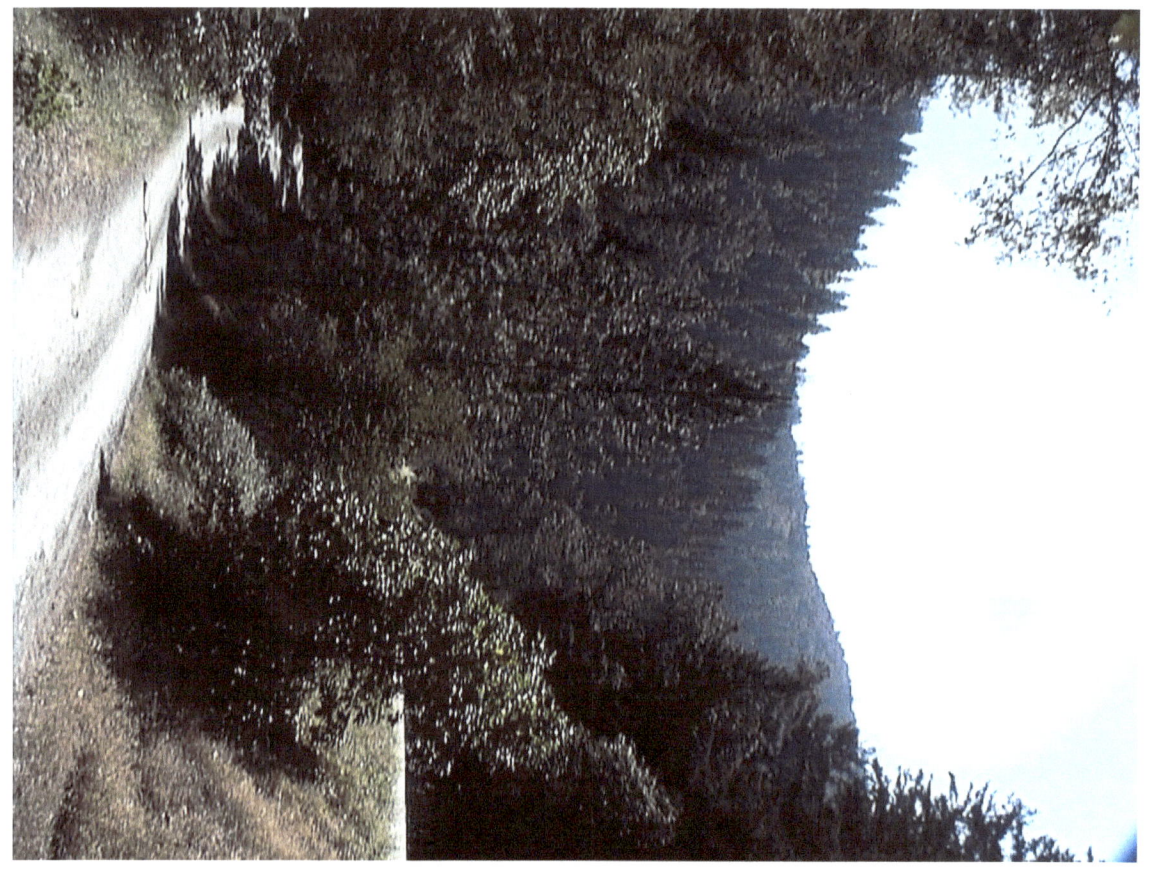

Pathway to Creativity

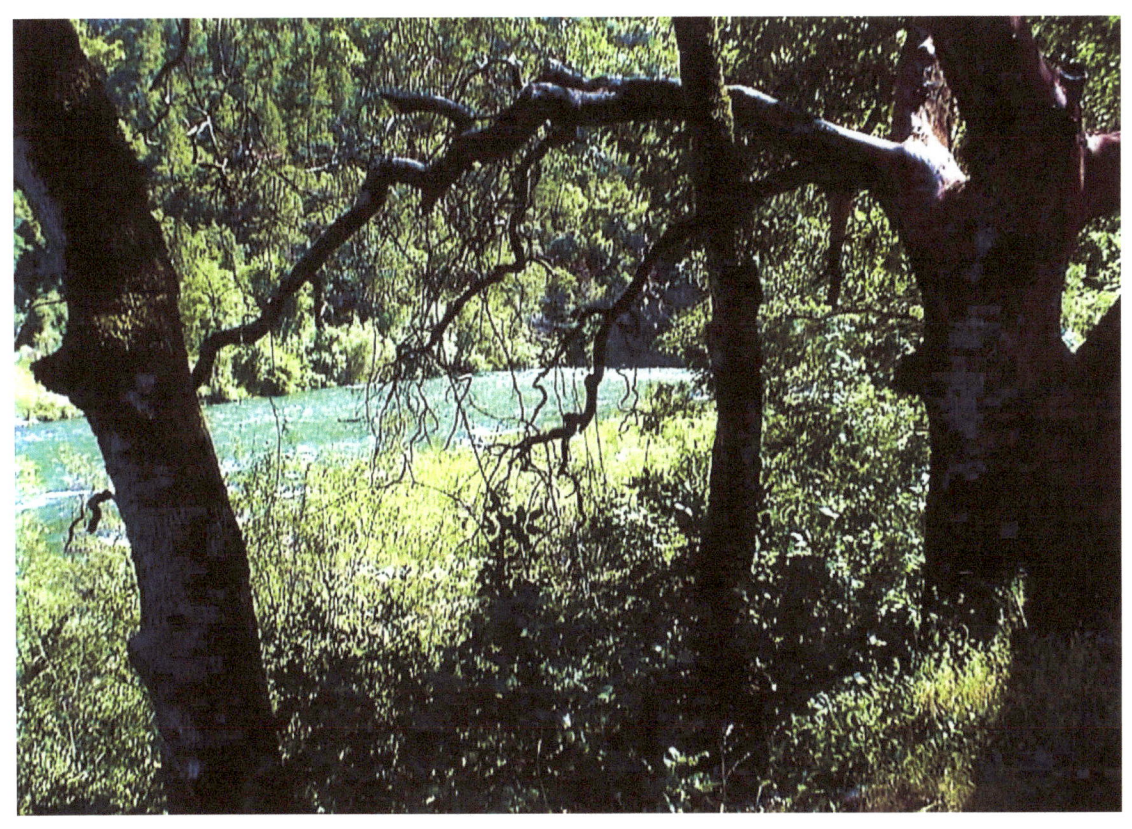

Inside Looking Out

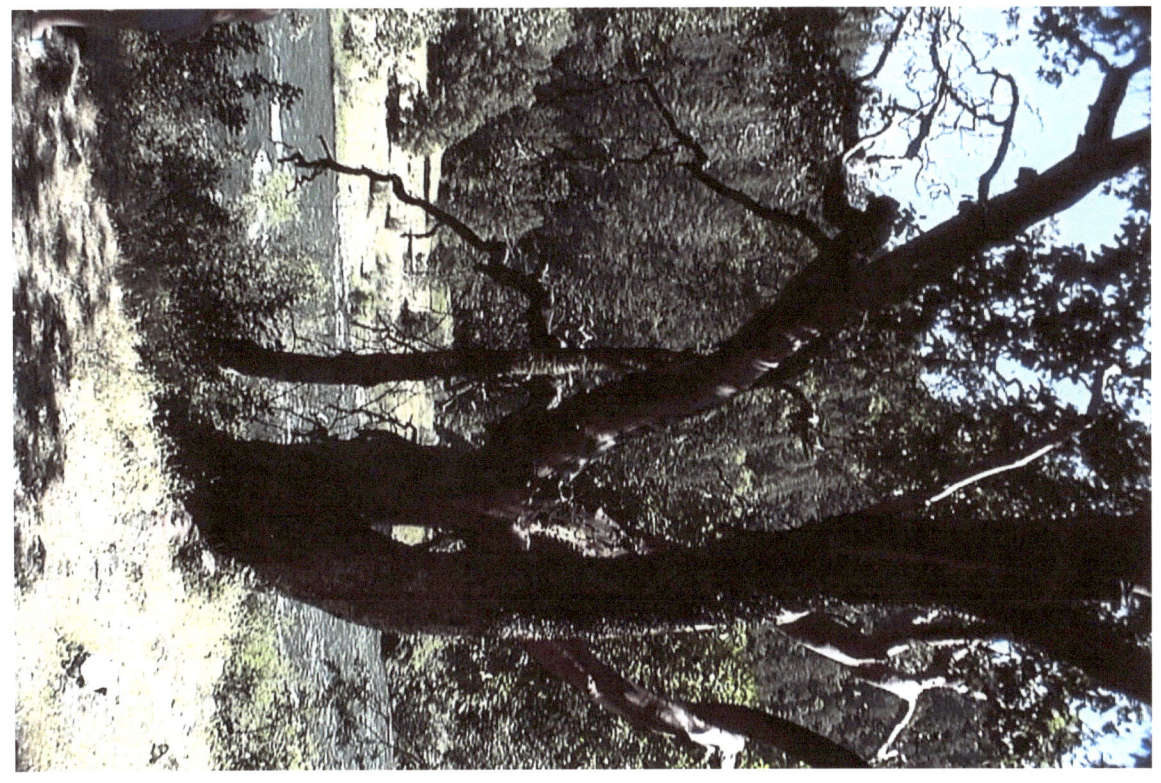

Seeing Roots

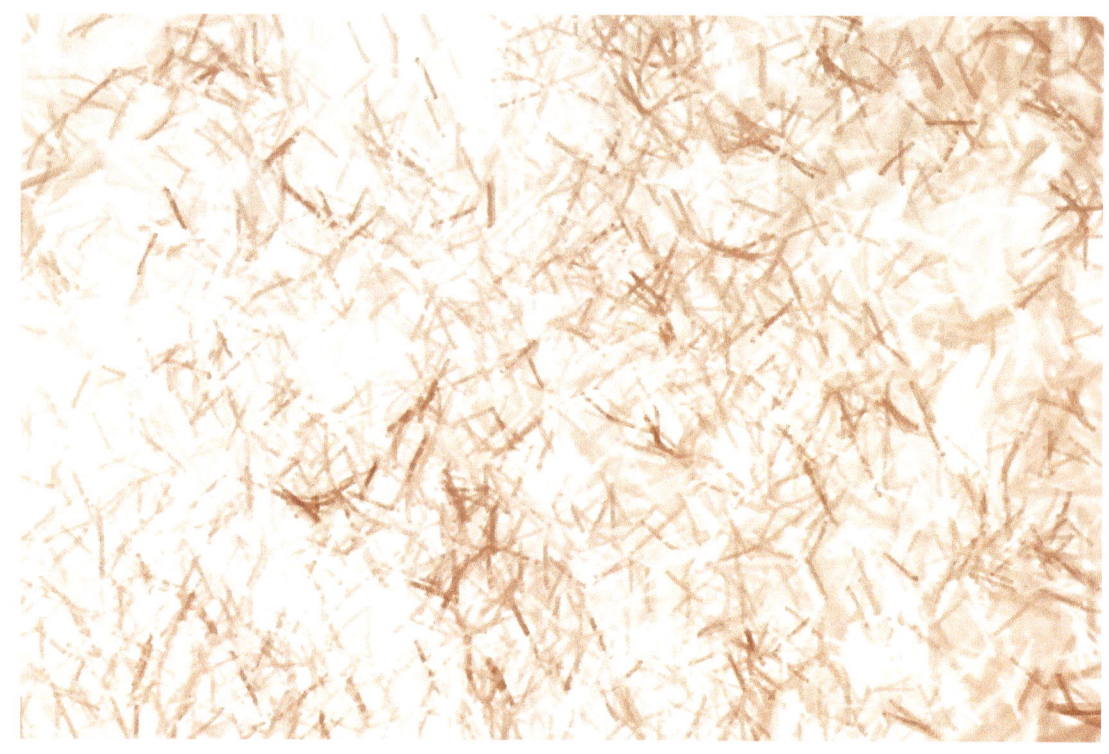

Placement

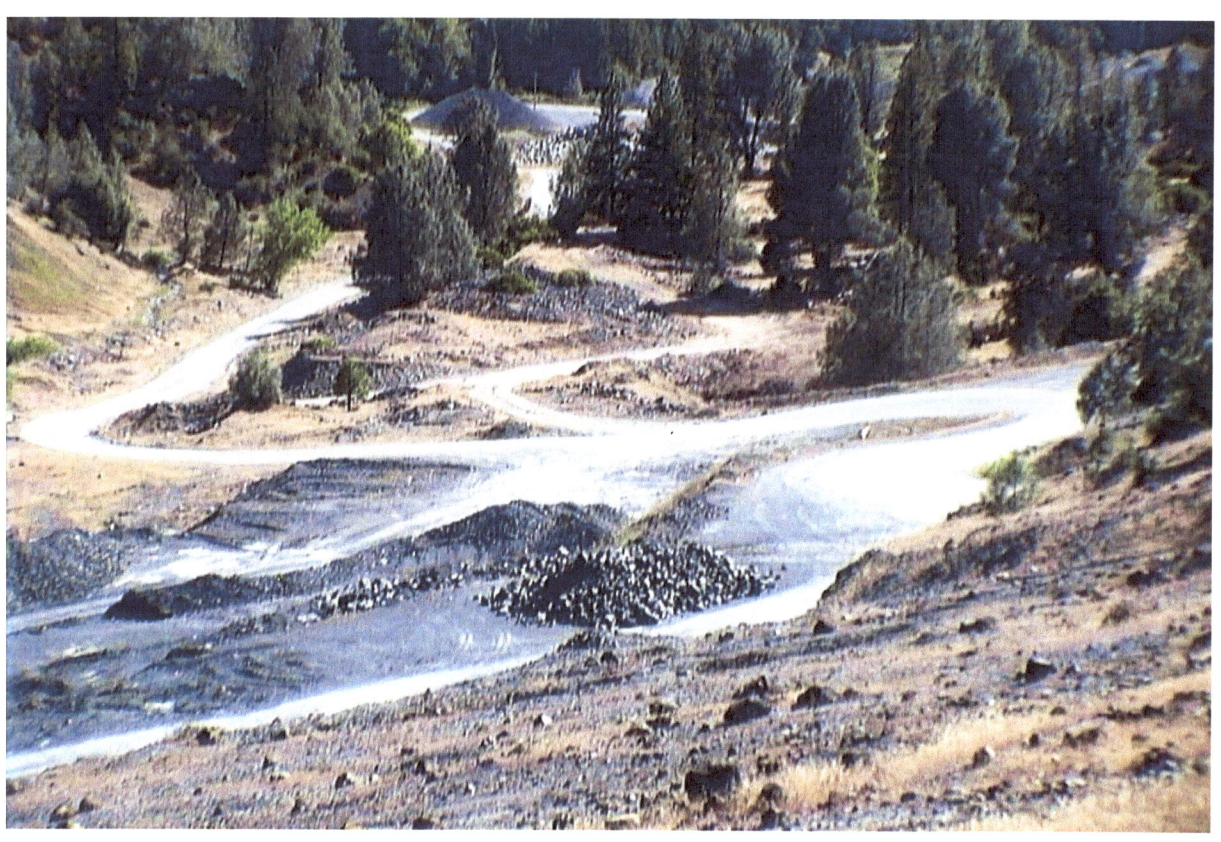

Focus Settlement

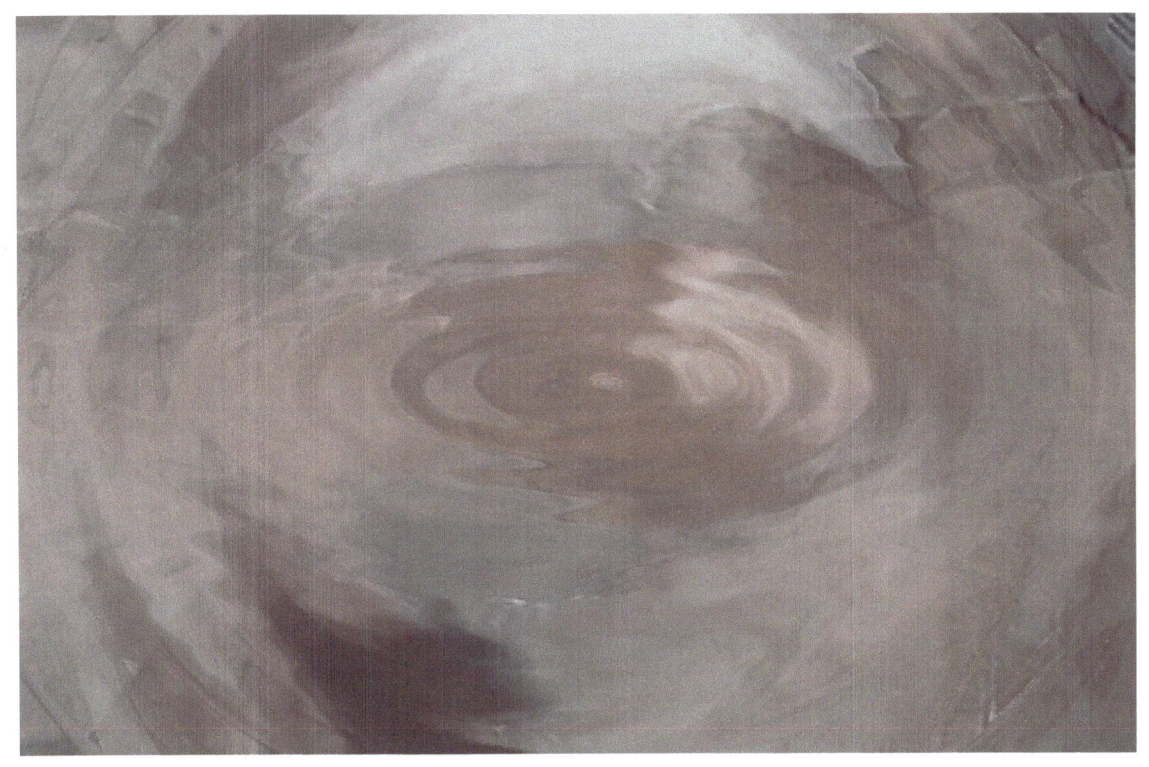

Finger Approach

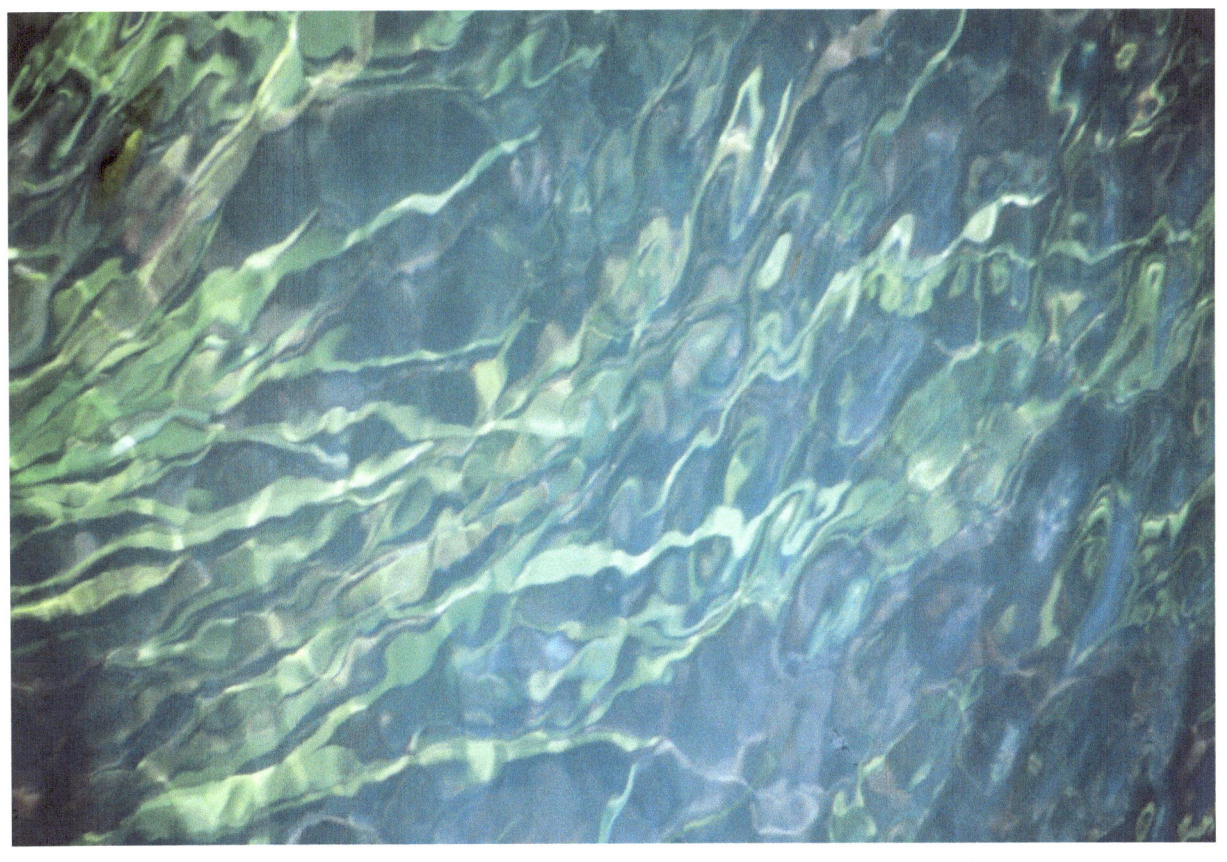

River Silkiness

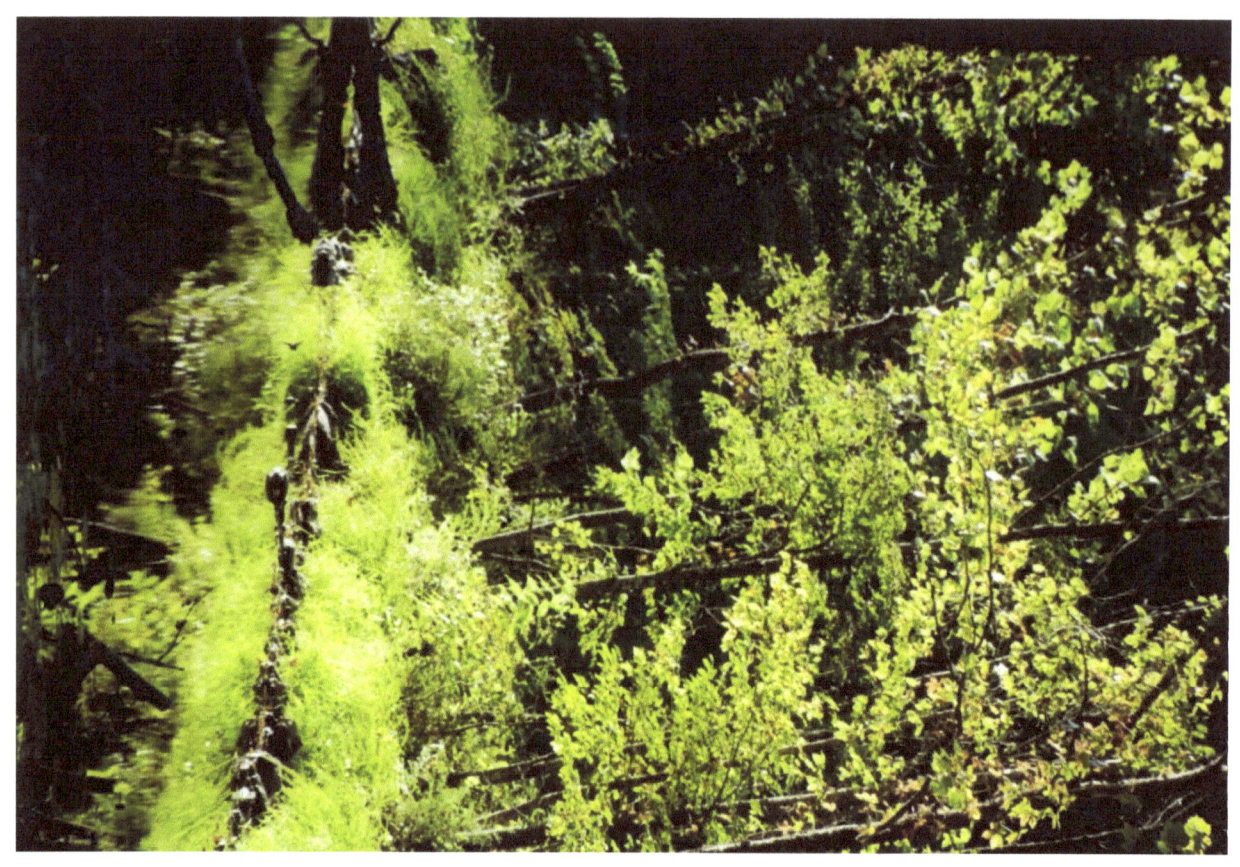

Gentle Pull

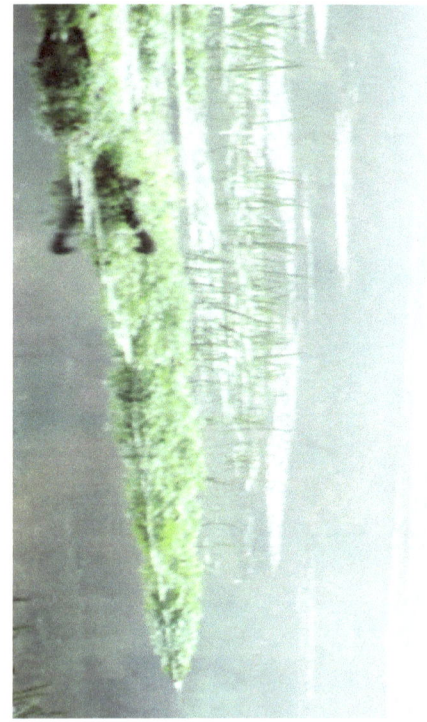 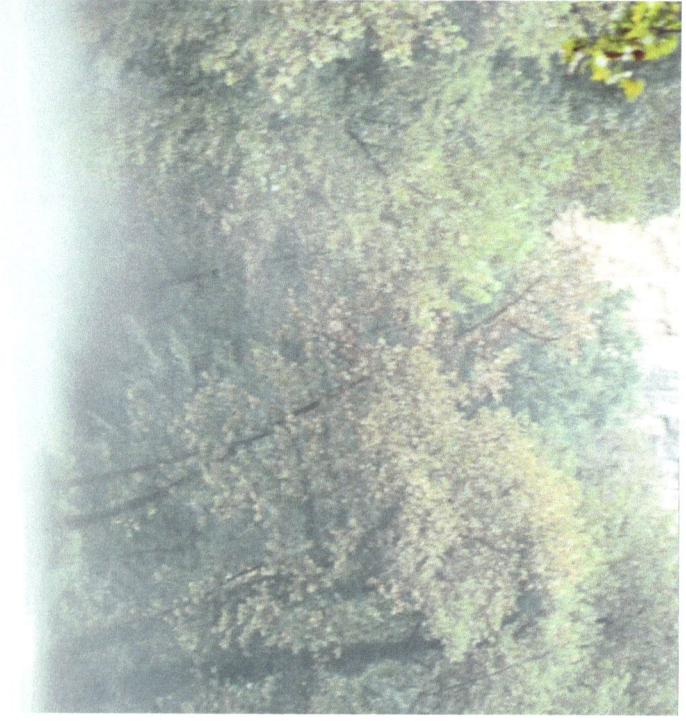

Pureness

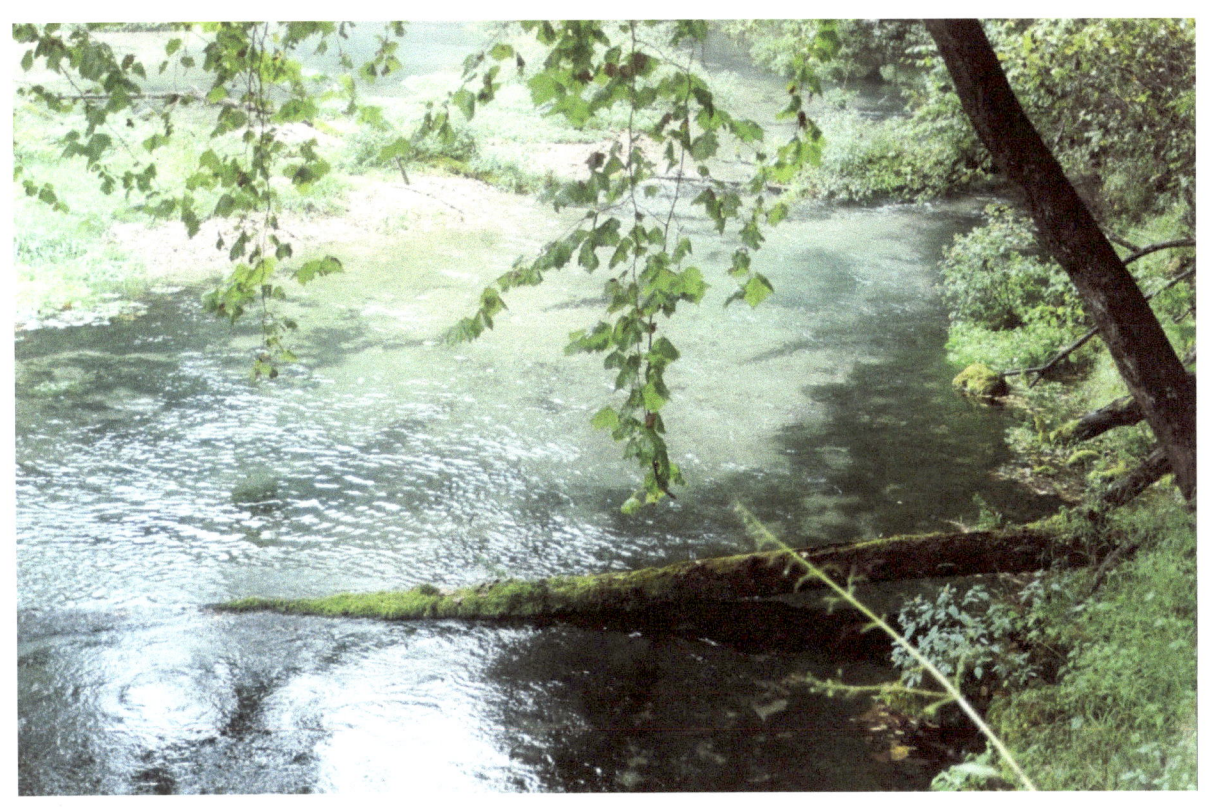

Surrender

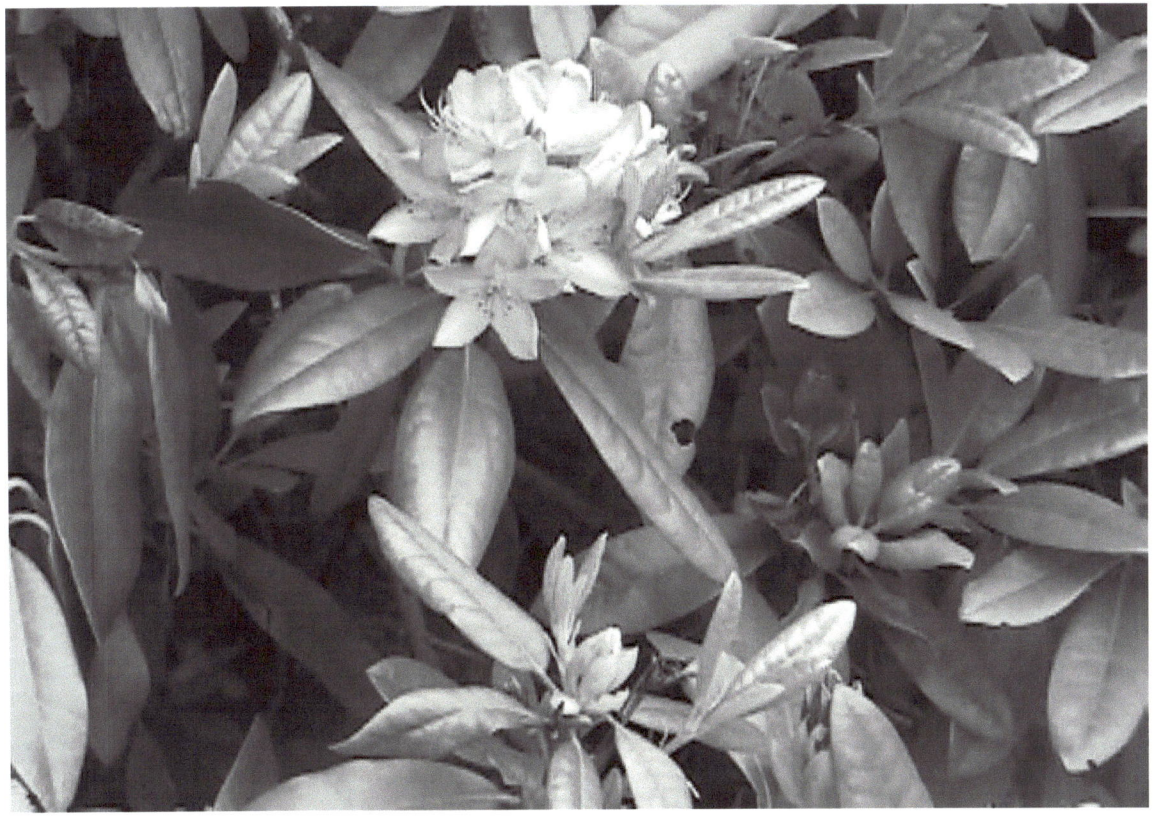

Holding On